The
Power
of
Wisdom™

The
MAGIC
of
SEEING
What
Others
CAN'T

The
Power
of
Wisdom™

The Truth
about
Your Money
and
Your Life

that your parents, teachers and mentors
didn't know to teach you

———————————————

The Wisdom Institute

THE **POWER** OF
WISDOM
The Magic of Seeing What Others Can't

ISBN 0-9671350-0-1
PUBLISHED IN THE UNITED STATES OF AMERICA by:

THE WISDOM INSTITUTE
P.O. Box 8004, Redondo Beach, CA 90277-8004

WARNING — DISCLAIMER

CONTENTS

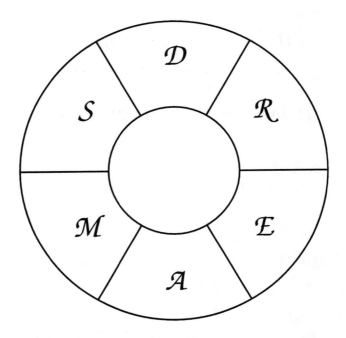

Where is the wisdom
we have lost in knowledge?

Where is the knowledge
we have lost in information?

T.S. Eliot

Introduction

This book opens the door to a whole new world for you.

A world filled with harmony, fulfillment and abundance.

A world without struggle and without confusion.

A world where success and accomplishment aren't a matter of how hard you work, or how much you know, or how much you own.

A world where success and affluence naturally flow towards you, even seek you out.

The world that awaits you on the other side of the door is called the Age of Wisdom.

The world in which we live today is often referred to as the Information Age.

Entering the Age of Wisdom is like entering a parallel universe. You can still see the chaos and confusion that reigns on the lives of those you left behind on the other side of the door. But you are now immune to the struggle, fear, and disappointment that plagues them.

That's because, from your new vantage point, you see things that others can't even begin to see, you understand things that others can't even hope to understand, you are aware of things that others can't even imagine.

And this different perspective, in and of itself, brings you major personal and financial advantages that others can't even dream of enjoying.

This book is your key to the door that takes you to the Age of Wisdom.

Just as a key nudges the tumblers that otherwise remain motionless inside a lock, this book nudges awake the wisdom that otherwise lays sleeping inside you.

It gives you the power to access your inborn wisdom — and lets it become a natural, effortless part of you, the way it was meant to be.

When you enter the Age of Wisdom, it's like turning the light on in a previously dark room.

Switching on the light suddenly illuminates everything. Entering the Age

2

of Wisdom suddenly makes everything clear.

And just as it doesn't matter how long the room has remained in darkness — a day, a week, a month, even years — in the Age of Wisdom, it doesn't matter where you've been or for how long.

In a few moments, you'll commence your journey through the door to the Age of Wisdom.

But before you cross the threshold, be aware:

Once you enter the Age of Wisdom, it may not be possible for you to ever go back.

The Age of Wisdom is a glorious place that fulfills everything your heart desires. For the first time, you see the world with a new clarity. And your life gets irrevocably transformed.

Of course, you do have the choice of returning at any time to the incessant drama of the Information Age.

But if you do, you will feel a heavy emptiness. Once you've experienced the calm fullness and the ebullient success of the Age of Wisdom, you won't easily erase its memory from your mind.

As you enter the Age of Wisdom, you'll leave behind the frenetic world of the Information Age.

In the Information Age, we are caught up in a flurry of activity.

We scramble to move forward, to accomplish our goals, to attain happiness.

We become unhappy even as we struggle to capture happiness.

In the Age of Wisdom, you have no need to scurry. That's because you see things differently. You see that success doesn't come from what you do, or even how much you do.

You no longer mistake activity for productivity.

You know that nothing can keep you from the success and happiness you seek simply because you have a different vision of how to seek them.

In the Age of Wisdom, you move beyond the overwhelming pressures of the Information Age.

In the Information Age, information gushes at us faster than we can absorb it. Change hurtles at us faster than we can cope with it. Communication piles on us faster than we can respond to it.

Everywhere, the bar gets raised higher and higher. Yesterday's breakthrough is today's target-to-beat.

At work, we're under pressure to deliver ever improving quality, ever faster service, ever lower costs.

At home, we're under pressure to become the perfect spouse, the ideal parent, the all-round, better-than-our-TV-counterpart human being.

From the Age of Wisdom, you gaze upon all these demands with unruffled equanimity. That's because you are able to see *what's really going on.* And this simple but powerful insight delivers you major advantages.

In the Information Age, we get lost in a futile dance to stay on top of the latest information, the newest techniques, the hottest gadgets.

We are burdened with guilt and anxiety about missing out ... about becoming obsolete ... about simply being left behind.

In the Age of Wisdom, there's no fear of becoming obsolete. That's because information gets quickly outdated; but wisdom is timeless.

In the Information Age, we feel trapped in a world that seems out of control.

To gain some semblance of control, we seek to control the events and the people around us.

But we seek to control what is intrinsically uncontrollable. Our environment cannot be changed, or halted, or even slowed down.

To gain some sense of direction, we feverishly follow the herd, the latest fads, the charismatic, self-proclaimed "experts."

But we seek answers where answers cannot be found.

We expend energy where our efforts are quickly dissipated.

In the Age of Wisdom, you are secure in the knowledge that the answers you seek will become readily visible to you, just as reflective road markers

It's a Myth:

This is
the Information Age

become progressively visible on a fogged-in highway.

In the Age of Wisdom, all you have to do is be willing to shut off the clutter coming from the Information Age, and be willing to listen to your internal wisdom.

You already possess this wisdom.

It already resides within you.

You were born with it.

You've just never been shown how to access it.

This wisdom is your own internal reference point.

Once you access it, you're almost automatically raised above the noise and clutter that surrounds you.

Just as there are seven colors in a rainbow, there are seven steps to learning how to access your wisdom.

Each step logically leads to the next one.

Each step builds upon the previous one.

Each step nudges your internal wisdom to wake up in a different way.

As you ascend each step, think of it as switching on the light to one more color on the rainbow spectrum. At the end of the seventh step, when all seven colors are lit, lies the combined effect of all seven colors ... enlightenment.

The journey to accessing your internal wisdom is a fascinating, glorious experience.

The more you access your wisdom, the more effortless it becomes.

Until eventually, you navigate effortlessly through the maze of life.

Come, let's embark on this wondrous journey ...

About
Wisdom …

This book is about becoming able to see, without delusion, what is true in life.

It is about looking at life *differently*.

Most people see what *they want to see.*

For example, there was a time in our history when we saw the sun as revolving around the earth.

Human beings have always had a need to see themselves as the center of the universe.

So, rather than looking at the earth *as it really is,* we chose to distort the truth. We created maps and laws to reinforce *our version* of the truth. And we rejected and outlawed those who disagreed with our "truth."

Most people delude themselves in this way even today.

They welcome any information that supports their beliefs.

And they discard any information that debunks their beliefs.

Unless such people first learn how to see, they shouldn't believe what they see.

Even people who keep an open mind can't see things the way they really are.

That's because their perspective is blocked, or limited.

For example, most people can't *see* that the earth is moving through space at the phenomenal rate of 64,300 miles per hour — or, that it is rotating on its axis at over 1000 miles per hour.

The reason most people can't see this incredible speed is because, from their vantage point on the earth, the ground is firm and steady.

Similarly, most people can't see that the earth is round.

In order to see that the earth is round, you have to look beyond your immediate surroundings towards the horizon. And to see that the earth is round without a doubt, you must move to a higher elevation.

It's a Myth:

Seeing
is
Believing

How you see the world creates the foundation for your life and your accomplishments.

If you see only what you want to see — if you choose to see only your own projection of the truth — you will build your life on a foundation of false assumptions.

And so, you will destine yourself to inevitably crumble. You will become so overwhelmed and confused, you won't know what to believe.

On the other hand, if you become willing to look at the world differently and see things as they really are, you will see the shortcuts around your obstacles even as you spot the obstacles. You will clearly see the opportunities that are always abundantly in front of you. You will expend your energies on what really matters.

Your success will depend not so much on what you do, but on what you see.

Your wisdom will ultimately create your wealth.

The Wisdom

of

Duality

Nature endows every person and every event
with a unique blend of characteristics,
finely honed for the fulfillment
of its own special purpose.

And when you see this exquisite whole
— without judging its individual components —
you get aligned with the ample abundance
nature intended for you

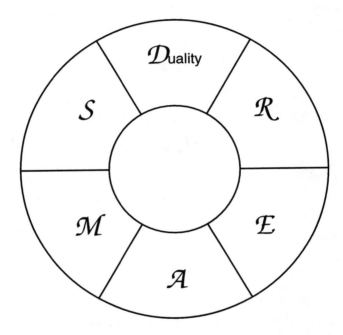

The test of a
first-rate intelligence is

the ability to hold
two opposed ideas in the mind
at the same time,

and still retain
the ability to function.

F. Scott Fitzgerald

The Wisdom of Duality is your first step into the Age of Wisdom.

It forms the foundation for fulfilling your dreams and collecting the accomplishment that nature intended for you.

The symbol of the Wisdom of Duality is a coin.

When we toss a coin up into the air, we always look for whether it comes up heads or tails.

The result of the toss — heads or tails — is clear, specific, precise.

This is the way we've all been trained to see, expect, and resolve everything we encounter in our lives.

We've learned to clearly identify whether something is heads or tails … black or white … good or evil … true or false … dark or light … strong or weak … hard or soft … win or lose … happy or sad.

In a sense, we've been *programmed* to look at our life, our situation, our circumstances as a series of dichotomies.

This is largely because the *physical* world around us manifests itself to us in such dichotomies.

For example, at the present moment, you are sitting on what is clearly a chair. There's no question about whether it is or isn't a chair. It simply and unambiguously *is* a chair.

It is easy to extrapolate this experience of the physical world to our entire universe of experiences.

And our upbringing has only served to reinforce this perspective.

That's because our parents, our teachers, and our mentors were themselves trained to look at the world in this polarized way.

Technological progress has further fortified our tendency to sort things into "either/or" buckets.

That's because computers employ binary logic. They require clear, precise input. And they output neat reports and black-and-white spreadsheets.

Technology lulls us into believing that all of life should be interpreted in this cut-and-dried way.

With the Wisdom of Duality, you *rethink* the *way* you think.

You learn to look at the universe *as it really is*.

The universe is *not* linear, *not* binary, *not* polarized.

To understand this, go back and examine that tossed coin again.

Allow yourself to see more than what you're accustomed to seeing.

While you're looking at the side of the coin that you can *see,* be aware that your coin has *both* heads *and* tails.

Heads and tails are merely two *aspects* of the very same thing. They are *inseparable* from each other.

Even though you *see* just one side of the coin, one side cannot exist without its opposite.

It is physically impossible.

If your coin comes up heads now, tails is just another toss of the very same coin away.

When you toss the coin, you have *no control* over *when* or *whether* it will come up heads or tails.

This simple change in perspective — from looking at just one side of the coin to expanding your field of vision so that you are aware of both sides, no matter which side is up — may appear inconsequential.

But it is very empowering.

And very liberating.

Because it puts you in harmony with the true nature of life — and the universe.

In the universe, the north pole exists *because* the south pole exists. And vice versa.

It is simply not possible for anything — a magnet, the planet earth — to have a north pole without *also* having a south pole.

Just as it is for the north pole and the south pole, just as it is for heads and tails, so it is for black and white ... for hot and cold ... for strong and weak ... for happiness and sadness ...

Each is merely a different manifestation of its opposite.

Each cannot exist without its opposite.

Each is indeed *dependent* upon its opposite.

This is the Wisdom of Duality.

With the Wisdom of Duality, you align yourself with the true course of nature.

It's a Myth:

What
you see
is
what
you get

And nature reciprocates by aligning you with your true — and optimum — course to abundance.

The Wisdom of Duality may also be called the Wisdom of Discernment.

That's because this wisdom allows us to discern between things the way they really are and the way we'd like to see them.

The world around us is so chaotic, so unpredictable, that we yearn to gain a sense of order and stability around us. This is why we sort things into clearly demarcated lines. This is why we write laws, policies and procedures. This is why we define norms of acceptable and unacceptable behavior. This is why we form organization charts, and groups, and associations, and families, and even nations. This is why we need maps and directories to sift through the morass of information.

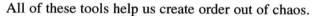

All of these tools help us create order out of chaos.

They also help us function socially.

These tools are vital to our survival ... and also, to our success.

Unfortunately, most people take these delineations too literally and too rigidly. They forget that these lines were *created by our mind* and have no basis in reality.

Nature does not share our need for clear boundaries.

Nature does not care that we draw lines on our maps to separate California from Nevada ... or the U.S. from Canada.

There is no fixed line of separation between the the ocean and the sand on the beach.

The most breathtaking sights in nature are visible, not at the peak of day or night, but at the confluence of the two ... dusk and twilight.

With the Wisdom of Duality, you are aware of the fundamental *social* need for dichotomies and boundaries and demarcations. But you are even more acutely aware of the ambiguous, amalgamated nature of life.

Most people's vision is restricted by a need for structure and order. They seek resolution and closure to the problems they encounter.

You have an open, enhanced vision of life *as it really is.*

You approach life's predicaments, opportunities and obstacles with a flexibility that matches nature's own fluidity.

As a result, you enjoy a liberated, expanded experience of life.

You move beyond the constant search for clarity and stability and security that unnecessarily bogs down the life of others.

17

Life is a struggle for for most people.

That's because they don't use their inborn Wisdom of Duality to guide themselves.

They struggle constantly to attain pleasure ... and then, *sustain* it.

And they struggle even harder to avoid *dis*pleasure.

But their struggle is futile. Because it is against the truth of nature.

When the Wisdom of Duality is incorporated into your consciousness, you can clearly and effortlessly — even spontaneously — see that pleasure and displeasure are inseparable.

You can see that, as you pursue pleasure, it's inevitable that you will encounter pain along the way.

That *true* pleasure never comes without sacrifice.

So, you no longer feel the compulsion to attain pleasure or to avoid displeasure. You no longer need to change or control your external environment.

Instead, you embrace each situation *as it happens*.

You become at peace and harmony and one with whatever happens.

You value each experience for its own sake rather than for the *feeling* it triggers.

You simply let the story of your life unfold. Indeed, you watch your life — your universe — with a sense of wondrous detachment.

Because you know, at a very deep level, that, each time the coin of your life gets tossed, you will "win" whether that coin comes up heads or tails.

Through years of linear thinking, we've come to believe that people who are "successful" possess some mysterious inborn attributes.

And that people who are "failures" lack those very same attributes.

With the Wisdom of Duality, you get aligned with the true origin of success and failure.

You accept success and failure as merely different sides of the same coin.

You recognize up front that, whenever you attempt something — in your home life, in your romance department, in your job, in your business — the outcome of that attempt is just as likely to be a "win" or a "lose."

And so, you know never to assign any *meaning* to success or failure, to winning or losing.

Success is not triggered by some mysterious inborn attributes.

It is triggered simply by a toss of that two-sided coin.

And just as the outcome of that toss is random, so is your success … and your failure.

But behind that randomness hides a very interesting process … and the *real secret to success.*

Each time you toss that coin *again,* you *geometrically multiply* your chance of experiencing success.

The more frequently you toss that coin, the more likely you are to experience success.

If you toss the coin just once, you have a fifty percent chance of experiencing success.

Toss the coin twice, and your chances of experiencing success at least once during these two tosses goes up to seventy-five percent.

Toss the coin three times, and your chances jump up to eighty-seven-and-half percent.

In essence, success is a game of numbers.

And the fundamental difference between those who enjoy enduring success and those who struggle with failure is that successful people *play* this numbers game.

And they play it *consistently.*

All salespeople experience rejection.

But unsuccessful salespeople give up after the first try, the first "no."

While successful salespeople keep trying.

They know that they may or may not get a "yes" on the first try ... or even the second try. But if they persist until the fifth try, they're almost guaranteed a "yes."

Successful salespeople never take a "no" personally because *it isn't personal.* It's just the Duality of nature playing itself out.

They know that they fail *only* if they stop trying, only if they *stop* tossing the coin.

If you want to attain worldly success, all you have to do is keep tossing that coin ... keep trying, even though you experience random bouts of short-term failure and short-term rejection ... keep trying, while cherishing and rejoicing those little "wins" ... until such time that the coin eventually and inevitably comes up a resounding "win."

If you have *already* attained worldly success, then it is especially important that you keep the Wisdom of Duality firmly in mind. Because the tide can and *will* turn on you the moment you stop tossing that coin, the moment you stop trying new and different things, the moment you become complacent.

And, if you have been an abject "failure" until today, take solace in the Wisdom of Duality. Because starting today, you can transform yourself into a sudden success simply by deciding to toss that metaphorical coin more frequently.

Because you really *can* go from failure to success overnight. Because this is what is intrinsic to nature.

The Wisdom of Duality brings you five wonderfully amazing side effects, all of which serve to tip the odds in your favor as you navigate through life.

First, it opens up a plethora of opportunities for you. On the surface, it may appear you are out of options. But in reality, *you are never out of options.* Your next big opportunity is as close as your next try, your next toss of the coin.

Second, the Wisdom of Duality makes you progressively adept, nimble, competent. That's because each time you try, you learn precisely *what* and *how* to try. And you become able to apply this learning to your next try.

Third, the Wisdom of Duality brings you a profound level of focus. Because as you keep tossing that coin, you gain a deep respect for the randomness of your outcome. This, in turn, transfers your focus from your outcome to the task at hand. You become able to immerse yourself in your task without ego and without fear.

Fourth, the Wisdom of Duality brings you the opportunity to learn more about yourself. As you learn to view your outcome with equanimity, you also learn to view yourself without judgement. This brings you clarity about how your own actions and behaviors may inadvertently be hindering your chances of success.

And fifth, the Wisdom of Duality makes you self-confident and adventurous ... ultimately, a magnet for success.

Because as you shift your emphasis from the outcome to the process, as you build faith in the process, you find yourself willing to take necessary risks. Which, in turn, harnesses big paybacks for you.

The Wisdom of Duality banishes the worry, the self-doubt, and the need to control that plagues most of us.

You *abandon* thinking about yourself, your ego, your shortcomings, or your environment.

Instead, like an athlete, you get so completely absorbed in what you're doing, you put forth your absolute personal best.

You become alive and energetic.

You feel a deep passion for the people around you, your goals and your life.

You are able to *both* <u>make</u> things happen *and* <u>let</u> things happen.

And even if your immediate outcome is not quite extraordinary, you *know* that you have the wisdom to inevitably collect it.

The result is nothing short of euphoric.

Compare this to the harried existence that most of us lead.

We are so *absorbed* in our own feelings that we fail to see that it's this very self-absorption that prevents us from getting what our heart desires.

Most people are obsessed with categorizing everybody — including themselves — according to their strengths and weaknesses.

But nature doesn't conform to this human obsession.

Every entity in nature has its own unique combination of strengths and weaknesses. These strengths and weaknesses are perfectly adapted to the individual environment.

If the situation is changed, a solid strength can suddenly deteriorate into a crippling weakness ... and vice versa.

For example, algae are the chief source of food for a variety of fish and underwater organisms. They are also a chief supplier of the earth's oxygen.

At the same time, algae produce a variety of different toxic compounds. Under certain conditions, these compounds can be poisonous to the fish that eat the algae and fatal to the humans who eat these fish.

With the Wisdom of Duality, you recognize the *coexistence* of strengths and weaknesses.

You go beyond the fantasy that people are either all good or all bad. Instead, you embrace each person for his *uniqueness*.

This doesn't mean that you ignore the other person's weaknesses.

It means that you look for ways to make these weaknesses work for you.

One way you do this is by getting the strengths of one individual to compensate for the weaknesses of the other. By putting these strengths and weaknesses together, you make the sum greater. Your differences serve to strengthen you.

Another way you do this is by moving the other person to a situation that matches his uniqueness ... a situation where his weaknesses become strengths. For example, moving a perfectionist to perform a task that requires meticulous attention to detail.

Most people place a high priority on being with friends and associates with whom they're "comfortable."

Bosses look for employees who "fit in" ... and don't "create waves."

Individuals seek friends who are "compatible" and share the same interests and outlook.

Without a healthy dose of opposite view points, such people are limited by their own narrow perceptions.

Their well-meaning friends and co-workers become *co-conspirators* in their own self-destruction.

Companies with managers and employees who are all very "agreeable" have a habit of walking off the cliff, because they fail to see the whole picture.

Individuals with "compatible" friends and advisors routinely make self-destructive — even self-sabotaging — decisions.

With the Wisdom of Duality, you deliberately go outside your circle of comfort.

You expand your circle to include "disagreeable" as well as "incompatible" friends. You cherish devil's advocates. You nourish mavericks.

You maintain a wholistic, more truthful vision of the world around you.

Most people scramble to cover up their weaknesses.

Some people attempt to cover up their weaknesses by designing their lives around taking care of the need of others.

Others design their lives around taking care of themselves, and expect the people around them to do the same.

With the Wisdom of Duality, you know that neither of these ways of relating to other people can be sustained for any reasonable length of time.

You know that true internal harmony comes when you take care of yourself, and *also* take care of the other human beings in your life.

Unfortunately, over the years, thousands of self-help experts and psychologists — in an attempt to wean us away from such unhealthy relationships — have urged us to "take care of yourself" ... "be true to yourself" ... "be independent."

And most people have internalized these messages by the tens of millions.

Yet, incorporating these messages into our lives has not eased our sense of disillusionment. Because the cure prescribed by these experts is just as one-sided as the original problem.

With the Wisdom of Duality, you know that independence is a state that cannot be sustained. Because everything is interconnected with everything else. And everyone is *inter*dependent on everyone else.

Everything and everyone coexists.

Most people hesitate to move to interdependence because taking care of your own needs *and* the needs of the people around you seems like a huge responsibility.

But wisdom is ultimately effortless. Your internal wisdom helps you see the path clearly ahead of you.

It simply and intuitively lets you *know* how to create and maintain harmony within your circle of influence.

As interdependence becomes a way of life, you attain the otherwise elusive sense of alignment, completion, satiation.

Because you get synchronized with the way nature intended your relationships and your life to be.

A simple reality of life is that practically everything we desire is in the hands of the people around us.

So, before we can fulfill any individual desire, we must first sell, coax, influence, inspire or negotiate with the people around us.

In other words, we must get the people around us to change their point of view and see things from our point of view.

To learn how to do this, most of us turn to books on selling techniques, negotiating tactics, and influencing strategies.

With the Wisdom of Duality, you get moved to the front of the race.

That's because, right at the outset, you *expect* the other person to have a *valid* opposite point of view.

So, you don't drown in the drama of proving you're right.

You start with the assumption that *both* points of view are right.

You respect the other person's point of view. You take the time to understand it. And then, you accept it, acknowledge it, and validate it ... without condemning it or judging it.

As the other person feels understood and accepted, he almost automatically gets into an open frame of mind, ready to make any reasonable changes.

Ultimately, you finish the race while most others are still trying to determine which ploy or tactic will work best.

Over the years, psychotherapists have drummed into us that "you can't control others" … "you can only control yourself."

With the Wisdom of Duality, you instantly recognize that this advice is only half true.

Because how a person responds to you is dependent on how you communicate with him.

Each time *how* you communicate sets the stage for *how* the other person responds.

You are not just the effect.

You are *both* cause and effect.

This is the reality of nature.

A chicken is both the result and the cause of an egg.

High tide follows low tide. It also yields to low tide.

With the Wisdom of Duality, you accept responsibility that another person's inappropriate behavior towards you is the result of your behavior.

You don't waste futile energy trying to assign blame.

Instead, you focus on modifying your reaction and behavior to create the effect you desire.

Therapists and consultants implore us to communicate with each other openly and freely, expressing our innermost thoughts, so that the people we care about are never left guessing.

They also encourage us to become empathetic listeners, explaining that this will help us understand and thus, bring us closer to the people important to our lives.

With the Wisdom of Duality, you know that this is a journey that can be fraught with frustration.

That's because each human being has ample sprinklings of both good and bad, both happy emotions and sad emotions, both clarity and confusion, both fear and fearlessness.

And this thick, intricate web changes with time and with situation.

With the Wisdom of Duality, you know that it's far more important to simply accept and love others — sharing their joys and being compassionate for their sorrows — even if you don't understand their innermost thoughts.

In 6th century B.C., Aesop taught us in his famous fable: *Don't kill the goose that lays the golden egg.* Instead, nurture it.

Because you need *both* the the goose *and* the egg.

Life is full of such predicaments where we are compelled to choose one thing over another.

Where, *no matter what we choose,* we know we'll have to give up key, life-nourishing benefits available only through the other path.

With the Wisdom of Duality, you know that thinking in dichotomies — choose one, give up the other — provides a temporary resolution at best.

Because it's only a matter of time before the rejected choice starts demanding our attention. And we end up with the predicament all over again.

For example, after years of being in an intimate relationship, many people start yearning for independence and freedom.

If they choose independence over intimacy, if they choose to move away from the relationship, it's a matter of time before they start yearning to fill up the resulting emptiness in their life once again.

If they choose intimacy and decide to stay in the relationship, try as they may, they remain unable to shake away the yearning for independence.

Such is also the case when a company has to choose between short-term profitability and long-term stability.

If the company chooses short-term profits, it rarely lasts long enough to enjoy these profits.

If the company chooses long-term stability, it can't generate the cash flow necessary in the short term to sustain its existence in the long term.

When your consciousness is open and aware of your Wisdom of Duality, then this *in itself* will guide you to a pathway that wasn't evident before ... a third pathway where *both options co-exist* ... a pathway which, without your internal wisdom, would have remained hidden and inaccessible to you.

With such a mutual pathway, you no longer have to sweat over the pros and cons of each option. You no longer have to agonize over what you must do without.

Instead, you become able to move forward with grace, rather than turbulence.

Spiritual leaders and contemporary advisors encourage us to "follow your heart," and "trust your instincts."

With the Wisdom of Duality, you know to pay attention to your heart and *also* to your head.

Instinct without the facts can be misleading.

Similarly, information can be meaningless without intuition and interpretation.

FOLLOWING YOUR
HEART

With the Wisdom of Duality, you know to first get at least the basic information before you can use your instinct to ignore it.

As Mark Twain once said, "Get the facts. And then, feel free to distort them."

Most people devote their entire lives to fending off other people's prejudices and biases.

They crusade to have these biases overcome.

Or, they resign themselves to being victims of these biases.

PREJUDICES AND
BIASES

With the Wisdom of Duality, you know that prejudices and biases are inherent in nature.

Nature is such a cauldron of opposites, most people aren't able to cope with its complexities.

So, in order to create order out of the chaos, they draw lines to distinguish one group of people from another. Inevitably, they choose the group *they* belong to as superior and the group *others* belong to as inferior.

This need to draw lines and distinguish is inherent in human nature.

Social intervention or government regulation may eradicate one set of lines. But it will soon be replaced by another set of new lines.

For example, in the U.S., minorities crusade for equality across race and gender. They want to erase the lines that separate them from their counterparts.

Yet, these same groups crusade to protect and maintain jobs within the country. They don't want corporations to export jobs to third world countries. They want solid laws to prevent mass immigration to this country. In other words, they want to draw solid lines between themselves and their human counterparts in other countries.

With the Wisdom of Duality, you simply choose to not participate in these divisive behaviors. You know that these lines are created in the mind and are not real.

So, you *act* as if these lines are not real.

You become neither the oppressed ... nor the oppressor.

And in doing so, you banish the mental boundaries that hold others back.

With your Wisdom of Duality, you see the needs of the people you left behind in the Information Age.

You see their need to create order out of chaos. You see their need to draw lines to distinguish one group from another.

And because you see these artificial lines so clearly, you also see how these lines can be put to work to bring maximum comfort to the people around you ... as well as major personal and financial fulfillment for yourself.

In the Information Age, people have a natural need to band together into groups, clubs, tribes and fraternities.

As global communications become easier, and the geographic lines separating people start getting erased, this need will intensify.

With your Wisdom of Duality, you can help people form such groups. But not along lines that increase discrimination. Rather, you help form groups that facilitate learning, adventure and camaraderie.

For example, Harley Davidson, the motorcycle manufacturer, and Saturn, the automobile manufacturer, have formed "tribes" of buyers. These buyers belong to fun clubs that help them socialize, share adventures, and become kids again. The payback for Harley Davidson and Saturn is loyal, repeat customers who become unofficial spokespersons for the company.

From time immemorial, human beings have been searching for the one best way, the one right answer, for handling each situation in life.

And to fulfill this yearning, every season a new crop of self-proclaimed gurus and experts and consultants sprouts up to share their "knowledge."

Most people follow the herd mentality. So, they blindly run in whichever direction such newfound gurus point them.

With the Wisdom of Duality, you know to listen with caution and skepticism to the one-sided proclamations of these overnight gurus.

For every profound truth, the *opposite* is also true.

There's no universal best way, no universal right answer.

What's best in one situation may or may not be best in another situation.

What's best for one person may or may not be best for another person.

And what's best for one person in a specific situation today may or not be best for that *same* person in that *same* situation tomorrow.

For example, the experts insist that people need to see and play with computers in a store before they'll buy it. Dell Computer achieved its tremendous success precisely by doing what all the gurus and experts in the computer business say can't be done. Dell sells its computers through mail order ads and the internet.

For a fourth of a century, the Wall Street Journal has been successfully using an advertising package that breaks all the established "rules" of advertising. The copy has no teasers, no promises, no proofs, no strong offers, no discounts, no urgency motivators. Yet, the package endures, pulling subscription orders year after year for the Journal.

In personal relationships, psychologists insist that the key to healthy relationships is communication. Yet, there is growing evidence, that unless it is used in the right situation, communication can actually make things worse.

Business schools emphasize the importance of preparing a business plan. They insist it is one of the keys to success. Yet, extensive research by the Entrepreneurial Research Consortium indicates that people with business plans are no more likely to succeed than people without such plans. Some companies start with massive business plans. Others start with no business plan. The business plan for Intel, the giant computer chip maker, was just one page.

Business schools also tout the pivotal role of market research. Yet, once again, for every success story based on extensive market study, there's another tale of triumph by a person who simply went with their gut.

At the bottom line, success paths are like fingerprints and snowflakes — no two are ever the same. Even though experts and gurus would have you believe otherwise.

With the Wisdom of Duality, you know that most of what gets passed out as the gospel truth is, in fact, little more than a bit of clever guesswork based on a few isolated experiences, packaged together appealingly so that it gets repeated over and over again until it takes the shape of a dogma cast in stone.

For example, psychotherapy is little more than an ideology. There has been no conclusive proof that any one branch of psychotherapy — including hypnotherapy and self-improvement — is more effective. Yet, because it is currently "in" to be in therapy, many people are quick to seek the "professional help" of a therapist.

With the Wisdom of Duality, you know that the "experts" who teach us right from wrong are themselves confused. They just don't *appear* confused because it's not in their best interest to do so.

You know that there's no such thing as objective advice. Every piece of advice is subjective, based on the advice-giver's limited perspective.

It's a Myth:

There is
one
right way!

Most people are always playing catch up.

This is because they read the same books as everybody else. They listen to the same consultants as everybody else. They launch the same initiatives as everybody else. They buy the same technology as everybody else.

And so, the only edge they can possibly gain over everybody else is speed.

He who gets first to the finish line of the latest initiative wins.

But he wins only temporarily. Because, as the competition inevitably catches up, everyone starts touting a new initiative or a new technology.

And the race begins all over again.

With the Wisdom of Duality, you know that success comes not from what you do, but from what you see.

Most people only see the rules that the experts preach.

You see that the opposite of these rules is also true. So, you *break the "rules."* When others zig, you zag. And so, you gain a substantial edge.

For example, the J. Peterman clothing catalog company has an edge over its competition *precisely* because it breaks all the rules.

Most clothing catalogs contain pictures of the clothes they sell. The Peterman catalog contains only line drawings and sketches.

The pages of most clothing catalogs are jam-packed with multiple items. The Peterman catalog typically shows only one item of clothing per page.

Most clothing catalogs emphasize the description of the clothing … such as fabric, size, and style. The Peterman catalog emphasizes the *romance* of experiencing the clothing in long-winded poetic fashion.

The Reiman company became one of the most successful magazine publishers in the country by targeting folks in rural America … while the rest of the publishers compete with each other in the urban arena.

Brylane became one of the most successful clothiers in the country because it targets "special sizes" … while Donna Karan, Gucci and Tommy Hilfiger compete with each other to clothe the fashionably trim.

In the health club field, Run N' Shoot has the market all to itself because it targets low-income communities while the rest cut each others' throats in middle- and upper-income neighborhoods.

WEALTH
WISDOM

Most people are inundated with new ideas, new concepts, and new fads.

They struggle to navigate through the overgrown jungle of new data, new gimmicks, new "technology."

With the Wisdom of Duality, you quickly sort through this morass.

You know that life is a unity of opposites.

And so, you become immediately alert when introduced to any new recommendation that is polarized or one-dimensional.

You know that every one-dimensional fad is at best, a half-way point to your goal ... and, at worst, something to be completely avoided.

You remain immune to the rantings of "experts" and "gurus" cajoling you to get on their one-sided bandwagons.

Thus, you forge ahead quietly and confidently, averting yourself from disappointments, frustration, self-rejection ... even as others are still struggling to make sense of the new information being crammed down their throats.

NEW FADS

The Wisdom of Duality provides some powerful — yet, ultimately simple — insights into the management fads of recent times.

For example, success with empowerment — a concept where managers must empower their employees to make decisions — has remained elusive and evanescent.

It has frustrated both managers and employees.

With the Wisdom of Duality, you know why a concept like empowerment — that *makes so much sense* — has failed in the real world.

You know that empowerment needs to co-exist with its opposite … which is leadership. It isn't a matter of choosing one over the other. Employees need *both* freedom *and* direction. They need to be *both* empowered *and* led.

The teachings of management "gurus" were flawed in the past because they taught only leadership.

And their teachings are flawed today because they insist that empowerment is the only game in town.

In a misguided attempt to embrace this latest fad, most managers have abdicated leadership.

And employees, thrilled to finally have a say, look at any and all managerial direction as interference.

Leadership, by itself, didn't work *effectively* before.

And empowerment, by itself, can't work *effectively* today.

Managers and employees must be trained that leadership and empowerment must co-exist.

This will liberate both groups.

Both groups have been wasting energy feeling frustrated and misunderstood and overwhelmed.

Now that very same vast resource of energy can be rechanneled to creating success.

Another recent management fad, consensus decision making, has failed for the same reason.

With the Wisdom of Duality, you know that consensus decision making must coexist with *individual* decision making.

There are times when everyone needs to get involved. And there are times when a single leader must firmly and decisively set the course.

Both the individual leader and the group need to recognize that, together, they will have to *instantaneously* move from one position to another *as the situation demands it.*

And that this two-pronged approach is not only okay, it is *necessary.*

Yet another example of a one-dimensional fad is the the craze for teams.

In the past, all of a company's rewards, training, nurturing were focused on the individual. That was one-sided and so, flawed.

Today, all this same attention has been switched to teams. This, too, is one-sided and so, flawed.

With the Wisdom of Duality, you know that, in order to have strong teams, you need strong individuals. So, *both* must be nurtured, *both* must be supported, *both* must be rewarded.

Other flawed management fads are the slogans, "the customer is always right" and "the customer is king."

With the Wisdom of Duality, you know that the customer is as often wrong as he is right. It's just not in your best interest to tell him so.

You also know that sometimes it pays to listen to your customer; at other times, it pays to *ignore* the customer.

The customer is excellent at telling you how you're performing in the short-term ... and what new things you must add to your product line.

But, often, your customer doesn't know what products or services he will embrace tomorrow. He's unable to envision the future. And so, he is likely to lead you astray.

An excellent example of this is the ubiquitous Post-It notes. Had 3M listened to early customers, they would have never brought it to market.

Most people go through life believing that there's a certain "best" way to be.

And they actively crusade others to join *their* bandwagon.

For example, some people are right-brained, feeling, emotional, artistic types.

Others are left-brained, cerebral, thinking, analytical types.

People who are primarily feeling types can't understand how anyone would want to go through life being a thinking person.

And those who are primarily thinking types would never trade places with a feeling person.

With the Wisdom of Duality, you rise above such skirmishes.

You enjoy a full life.

You combine emotion with insight.

You can be both immature and mature, playful and disciplined, responsible and irresponsible.

Those who observe you have difficulty labeling you, because you can be both humble and proud.

You are proud of your own talents. Yet, you also have a humble respect for the hand fate plays in your success.

Most people try to make do with what they have.

But you are not only satisfied with what you have, you create a fuller, richer life for yourself by finding your *opposite* in the persons around you.

In your close friends and particularly your life partner, you look for characteristics you couldn't possibly have yourself.

In your career, you look for individuals that complement, rather than supplement, your skills.

While most people live their entire lives with the equivalent of only half a brain, you tap both sides of your brain.

You enjoy the full spectrum of logic *and* intuition; impulse *and* analysis; fantasy *and* reality.

With the Wisdom of Duality, you know that your optimum path lies where you combine the best of both your worlds.

In selling, salespeople who are both task-oriented *and* people-oriented earn fifty percent more than those who tend towards either extreme.

In politics, Bill Clinton won his reelection by combining the best of Democratic *and* Republican ideals, and creating a third, immensely powerful position, through a process he calls *triangulation*.

At home, families that play together and grow together *and,* at the same time, nurture each member's individuality, tend to stay together.

In business, companies that sell good, quality products packaged *with* a high level of service (call it *prodices*) outsell those who don't. For example, automobile companies that sell their cars packaged with 50,000-mile warranties, roadside assistance, and a free car wash with every tune-up have a distinct edge.

One retailer (Kohl's) found a way to sell name brands at discount-store prices. And they're blazing a trail ahead of *both* types of competitors — the discounters like Wal-Mart *and* the name-brand retailers like Sears.

Companies that cooperate *and* compete with their competitors (call it *coopetition*) have a distinct edge in the marketplace. That's because such companies, though fiercely competitive, are not shy about collaborating with specific resourceful competitors to create breakthrough new technologies that leave *all other* competitors in the dust.

Opportunities are abundant for those who combine order with chaos (call it *chaorder*). And those who do are often substantially more successful and more profitable than other players in that market.

VISA integrates an international network of banks that accept all VISA credit cards, issued by *any* bank in the network (order). Yet, all participating banks in the network compete with each other for credit-card customers, and each bank offers its own portfolio of rates and services (chaos).

TV Guide integrates a growing network of TV, cable and satellite options (chaos) into a well-organized weekly schedule (order).

J.D. Powers & Associates does the same thing for automobiles.

Zagat Surveys does the same thing for restaurants.

And 1-(800)-FLOWERS does the same thing for flowers.

As new technologies get introduced into our lives at breakneck speeds, most people fall into one of two camps:

They either actively pursue the new technologies.

Or, they vigorously defend the old technologies.

With the Wisdom of Duality, you recognize that both the old and new will coexist for a long time, perhaps even forever.

Highways changed how we travel. But they didn't eliminate the locomotive.

TV changed how we get entertained. But it didn't banish movies or radio. Both movies and radio are still immensely profitable.

Computers changed how we share information. But, instead of creating a paperless society, it has triggered a boom in paper demand.

The internet is changing how we communicate. But it won't soon replace the telephone. Because, even today, nine out of every ten households on the planet do *not* have a phone.

And this is the way of nature.

Because, in nature, as new species evolve, and other species become extinct, several decades or centuries pass while both species coexist.

Most people bury their head in the sand. They ignore the coexistence of the old and the new.

But the most successful people acknowledge this reality and then, use it to guide their actions.

For example, SouthWest Airlines achieved its legendary success by acknowledging the existence of the automobile. SouthWest realized it wasn't just competing with other airlines. It was competing with automobiles as well. So, it set its fares to be competitive with automobiles.

The Wisdom of Duality makes you aware of the coexistence of opposites.

At its core, it makes you aware of your options. And it helps you see a new, third option for every pair of options.

But all these options can be both a blessing and a curse.

YOUR FUTURE

It's a blessing because you can see things others can't even begin to see.

It can be a curse unless you know how to act on what you see.

With the Wisdoms of Resonance, Ecology, Aggregation, Magnanimity and Stratification, you'll see how to act on what you see.

Accessing
THE WISDOM OF DUALITY

(1)   Today, I will review my every emotion, my every decision, my every action to make sure it isn't too one-sided. Am I giving adequate consideration to the opposite side of the coin? Am I holding both sides of the coin in equal and clear perspective?

(2)   I will also review every advice, every guidance, every direction given to me by others. Is this advice too one-sided? Where is its opposite? How can I align this guidance with what nature intended?

The Wisdom

of

Resonance

Everything in nature
is alive, pulsating,
constantly resonating to and from the ideal,
but always missing the mark.

And when you see
the might and inevitability of this resonance,
you set into motion
the inevitability of your own success.

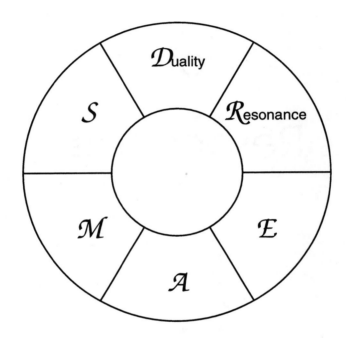

*Life is like
a blanket too short.*

*You pull it up
and your toes rebel,*

*you yank it down
and shivers meander about your shoulder.*

Marion Howard

The Wisdom of Duality — using the evocative symbol of a coin — is a powerful and necessary instrument for accessing your internal wisdom.

By switching on the first light in the room of your mind, it allows you to see things in a completely different way. It gets you to rethink the way you think.

The Wisdom of Resonance switches on the second light and reveals a new perspective and dimension, thus fortifying your ability to collect the accomplishments you desire.

The symbol of the Wisdom of Resonance is a string, four or five feet long, tied at one end around a coin.

When the string is held from its free end, the coin swings like a pendulum.

As the pendulum swings, each of the two high points in its path — the extreme points where the pendulum momentarily stops before changing direction — represent the opposites of the Wisdom of Duality … the black and white … the hot and cold … the win and lose … the strong and weak …

The position where the pendulum is at rest and completely still — and the string is standing perfectly vertical — is the amalgam of these two extremes. This is the point where both extremes mutually co-exist.

The pendulum rarely *stays* at this ideal, resting position.

The slightest change — even the ever so slight change in air currents caused by a person walking across the room — can cause the pendulum to start gently swinging away from its perfectly vertical position.

If someone touches the string, in an attempt to get it to stay still, the touching in itself causes the pendulum to swing more … sometimes even erratically and turbulently.

This is the essence of the Wisdom of Resonance.

Even after you've identified the "perfect" state where both opposites co-exist, the simple reality is that it's next to impossible to actually attain this state for any significant period of time.

Sometimes you get close to it. Sometimes you remain far from it.

Most of the time, you're moving either *to* it or *from* it.

Even when you finally reach it, something totally out of your control sets you off track again.

99.9999999999999999+ percent of the time, you're never quite at the "perfect" state.

So, 99.9999999999999999+ percent of the time you feel the uneasiness of being "wrong." You feel the pull to change directions. You feel the guilt of not giving it your all. You feel the impending sense of "failure."

All because you're not quite where you know you should be.

This is the reality of life.

And this is the reality of nature.

We all seek balance in our lives.

But in nature, there's no balance, no state of equilibrium, no sense of stability.

In nature, perfection doesn't come from *being* at a perfect, balanced state.

Perfection comes from resonating beautifully and harmonically and peacefully *to* and *from* the ideal state.

In nature, nothing is static. Everything is dynamic, resonating, pulsating, oscillating, wiggling, flirting.

The weather is constantly changing, continuously seeking its perfect balance.

Tornadoes, floods, snow-storms, famines, earthquakes … all are attempts by nature to reach that ideal state of balance, but always missing the mark.

Sometimes, nature misses the "mark" by a large degree. And this results in hurricanes and volcanic eruptions.

Sometimes, nature gets close to the "mark." And this results in awe-inspiring beautiful blue skies, spotted with fluffy clouds.

But the cycle of nature never stops.

It always continues, to and from, but never quite attaining the ideal state.

This is the natural order of things.

This is the way things *are*.

This is reality.

It's a Myth:

Balance means equality, equilibrium, stability

Everything else is simply our own *projection* of reality.

Most people choose to be guided by their own projection of reality. They choose to focus on the fact that they are *not* at the ideal, "perfect" state, never realizing that 99.9999999999999999+ percent of the time, it's impossible to be at that state.

And so, they doom themselves to a life of despair and inadequacy.

With the Wisdom of Resonance, you see things the way they really are.

Your compulsion to set things "right" evaporates. Your struggle to control vanishes.

And this, in itself, reduces the commotion in your life geometrically.

Because once *you* stop interfering with the harmonic swing of your life, once *you* just let things be as they *have* to be, you remove the biggest source of agitation in your life.

Ultimately, you reach a state where your life just swings synchronously, effortlessly, frictionlessly.

And you become able to devote your time, money and energy to enjoying life — and its rewards — in totality.

One of the great myths perpetuated by the Information Age is that it is possible to "balance" our lives.

And when most of us decide to balance our lives, we do it with the expectation that "things will soon get better."

Individuals lay this expectation on themselves and their families.

Managers broadcast these expectations to their team and their coworkers.

But nature never quite allows things to reach the idyllic "better" state. It constantly oscillates to and from it, ever getting closer to it, but never quite reaching it or resting at it.

Since we are not prepared for this reality, we soon get disillusioned, burned-out, and increasingly reluctant to start new initiatives.

The Wisdom of Resonance applies to diets. It also applies to the crusade for equality for women, minorities and gays. It comes into play when a person decides to balance his life between the polarized demands of work and family. And it's ever present whenever you implement a change at home or in the workplace.

With the Wisdom of Resonance, you know to align expectations with reality.

For example, a company that wants to implement empowerment in the workplace must help managers and employees see the duality of empowerment *and* leadership.

Then, they must help everyone see the resonance between leadership and empowerment. Otherwise the company will experience a high degree of burn-out among both managers and employees.

This is because there will be times when the *sensation* will be that one has won out over the other ... such as when an employee occasionally exceeds bounds, or when a leader occasionally takes charge.

With the Wisdom of Duality, you traded in your single lens for a bifocal lens, with which you can now see opposites together.

With the Wisdom of Resonance, you upgrade to a multi-dimensional lens, with which you can see opposites *as well as* the whole spectrum of everything in between.

All of us are striving to make our lives better.

In our personal lives, we strive to look better, lose weight, adopt new habits.

In our careers, we strive to learn new skills, get new responsibilities and big promotions.

In our businesses, we aim to boost our profits, slash our costs, implement new systems.

Yet, the Wisdom of Duality says that the old way and the new way, the old habits and the new habits, the old systems and the new systems will, by nature, tend to coexist.

And the Wisdom of Resonance says that not only will the old and new coexist, things will inevitably yo-yo back and forth between them.

This is the experience of most people who go on a diet. They find themselves constantly swinging between periods of dieting and splurging.

This is also the experience of companies implementing a new procedure or a new system. The tug of the old system never goes away. And the company finds itself quickly split into two factions, with one faction crusading for the new system and another faction subversively fighting to bring the old system back. From moment to moment, activity to activity, the company as a whole never quite knows which system is being used.

This can be tremendously frustrating, especially when you want to *deliberately* move from an old way of doing things to a new way of things.

Because the natural forces want the old and the new to co-exist and resonate back and forth.

Once again, nature provides clues …

In nature, new beginnings are created through an act of destruction.

It takes a massive act such as a volcanic eruption or a major hurricane or a shattering earthquake to wipe out the old and create an environment where new life can flourish.

CONSTRUCTION
AND DESTRUCTION

So, when it is your desire to move from an old order to a new order of things, you must deliberately destroy the old in order to be able to construct the new.

For example, most people attempt to quit cigarettes by smoking one less cigarette every day. They attempt to diet by eating slightly less every day. Such attempts are doomed to fail because they violate the intelligence of Resonance.

When you decide to go on a diet, in order to stick to it, you have to kill and bury your past image of yourself. The old "you" can no longer exist in your mind. Otherwise, you'll easily slip back and start yo-yoing again.

When you embark on a new project to increase your income, you have to know that the person who used to whither his time away watching TV, or procrastinating, or chasing empty dreams no longer lives.

A company implementing a new system or procedure has to burn all bridges back to the old systems so that everyone clearly knows that there's no going back.

Every new beginning must be preceded by an ending.

Every act of construction must be preceded by an act of destruction.

And *you* have to initiate the destruction. *You* have to kill your past. Otherwise, you'll waste an inordinate amount of time, money and energy without making any real progress.

Most people are averse to taking drastic action because they feel insecure about the future.

So, they tiptoe into change.

But with the Wisdom of Resonance, you know that, if you want a fundamental change to *stick,* you must ride the crest of the change.

Like a surfer in danger of being swallowed up if he moves too cautiously, you must move swiftly and boldly.

Big, bold changes have a string of advantages ...

Big changes are more likely to stick than small changes because big changes capture everybody's imagination and enthusiasm.

Big changes often bring sweeping and swift results.

Big changes carry so much momentum that they pull the support of those who'd otherwise remain on the fence.

Big changes also pull together everybody who has to wade through the crisis.

Big changes trigger an avalanche so powerful that the momentum carries you forward with gusto.

But big changes also have one important drawback: *there's no going back.*

So, you must have the wisdom to *see* your future *before* it's too late to go back.

And you can see your future through the Wisdoms of Ecology and Aggregation.

Accessing
THE WISDOM OF RESONANCE

(1)   Today, I will review all my expectations. Do I accept the reality that I will rarely achieve the so-called ideal of each of these expectations? Have I made this abundantly clear to myself and those around me?

(2)   Today, I will also review those goals where I have to close an old chapter in order to make it possible for me to start a new chapter. Do I clearly see that this is the only way I can rise to the higher plateau? Have I made it clear to myself and others that going back to the old chapter is not an option?

The Wisdom

of

Ecology

Nature operates through
a dynamic energy and tension
to keep everyone and everything
in synchronous harmony.

And seeing this tension
harnesses its immense power,
and triggers an avalanche
of success and accomplishment.

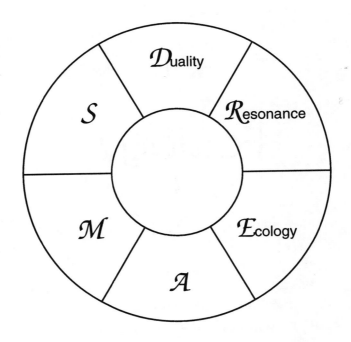

So many formulas
for success

carry a sting
in their tail.

Charles Handy

The Wisdom of Ecology switches on yet one more light inside the room of your mind.

With it, you see the true nature of the relationship between you and your surroundings.

You see *what's really going on around you.*

Unlike most people who look at their world with worry, fear and anxiety, you gaze upon your environment with equanimity.

This is why the Wisdom of Ecology is sometimes also called the Wisdom of Equanimity.

The Wisdom of Resonance sheds new light on the Wisdom of Duality. In the same way, the Wisdom of Ecology sheds new light on the two Wisdoms that were lit up before it.

The symbol of the Wisdom of Resonance was an extension of the symbol of the Wisdom of Duality. In the same way, the symbol of the Wisdom of Ecology is an extension of the symbols of the prior two Wisdoms.

The symbol of the Wisdom of Ecology is the same as the symbol of the Wisdom of Resonance — the mind-expanding pendulum — only it's turned upside down.

The symbol of the Wisdom of Ecology is a weight with a string attached to it. But this time, the weight pulls the string *up* — away from the earth — rather than down.

The symbol is a helium balloon with a string attached to it.

The balloon represents your desires, your goals, your dreams.

This may be material dreams, such as a new car or a larger home.

It may be financial dreams, such as more money or a successful business or a better return on your investment.

It may be professional dreams, such as a promotion or recognition or a better job.

It may be spiritual dreams, such as happiness or success or the feeling of being loved.

Or, it may simply be a dream of changing things from the way they are today … such as getting married if you are single, or getting divorced if you are married.

It is intrinsic to the nature of things that as you hold on to the balloon

— which is your dream — you experience a slight *pull* on the string. This is the tendency of the balloon to slip away and fly away from you.

You also have to exert an equal and opposite pressure on the string. This is the energy you must expend to hang on to the object of your desire.

This two-way force is the way of nature.

This tension is the glue with which nature holds everything together.

And this energy is the essence of the Wisdom of Ecology.

Ecology is the relationship between you and your environment.

And when the Wisdom of Ecology is incorporated into your vision, you see that nature connects you to your environment through a dynamic, life-infusing energy.

In the scheme of nature, nothing — no breathing being, no living organism, no cell, no atom, no electron, no planet — exists in its environment without a palpable, continuous tension.

This tension is *necessary* for survival.

It is how everything is connected with everything else.

It is the reason why things are the way they are.

The earth would not rotate around the sun — the earth would not *exist* — were it not for the continuous tug of gravitational forces between it and the sun.

A molecule would not exist were it not for the centrifugal pull between its electrons and its nucleus.

A magnet would not be a magnet were it not for the opposing forces between its north pole and its south pole.

This tension exists in perpetuity.

In all things.

Everywhere.

It is the foundation of life and the universe.

When you see this energy in its true pure form, and embrace its existence, it becomes your ally.

And your wisdom shepherds you through to the fulfillment of your dreams and desires.

But in the Information Age, we tend to deny the existence of this essential energy. What we don't realize is that we struggle against the fundamental intention of nature. And so, we unleash an infinity of turbulences into our lives, never realizing that our frustrations and our disappointments are our own creation.

In the Information Age, we're constantly assaulted by images and messages that tell us that *the way things are* just isn't good enough.

We're seduced by the promise of a better body, a better job, a better income, a better relationship, a better life.

We get enticed into a non-stop dance to acquire the latest information, the newest techniques, the hottest gadgets.

We are burdened with guilt and anxiety about missing out, about becoming obsolete, about simply being left behind.

And so inevitably, we get shrouded by a cloak of boredom, resentment, inadequacy.

With the Wisdom of Ecology, you gaze upon this dance with unruffled equanimity. That's because you see the pull of the new in an entirely different way.

It's as though you get transported behind the scenes into the projection room. And you vividly realize that the fantasies projected by the Information Age are a natural instinct, a necessary tension.

You recognize that, on the surface, no job, no income, no relationship is innately satisfying.

So, even though you experience the sensation of unrest and discontent, this feeling, *by itself,* doesn't govern your actions or your decisions.

As you see the reality, your heart opens up and feels a deep gratitude and joy for your life *as it is.*

You perceive its power and its beauty, despite its ordinariness.

You no longer fear becoming obsolete. You're no longer afraid of the novelty wearing off.

You are aware of the tension. But you are not unsettled by it.

When you view your environment through the prisms of Ecology and Duality, a new window opens up and allows a brighter light to shine in.

You see *both* the draw and attraction of the new possibilities ... *and* the fine rewards of your existing environment.

You are curious about the new. Yet, you have a deep sense of gratitude for the present *in its every detail.*

And this unique perspective sets the stage for a life of abiding and abundant joy.

In the Information Age, we are inundated with messages from every direction that there *is* an escape from the ever-present tension of our environment.

Even religious institutions, spiritual groups and therapy practices join the great delusion.

And not knowing better, we rush into their open arms, hoping to be rescued.

But our tension only deepens as we eventually realize that these forms of escape are temporary as well.

With the Wisdom of Ecology, you finally see that your only effective alternative is to accept the reality of the universe, and to allow this acceptance to generate its power for you.

Religion, spiritual practice and therapy — when dedicated to awakening your wisdom — can be an important means of transportation towards personal enlightenment.

Unfortunately, they are usually oversold as *the* destination.

In the Information Age, it's easy to simply dismiss the familiar and the ordinary. It's difficult to get excited about something unless it's new, or more, or faster, or bigger. It's exciting to believe the hype of the perfect job, the perfect lover, the perfect income.

But in nature, nothing exists in a tension-free environment.

Weeds always return to a garden no matter how well you eradicate the weeds. The job of weeding is never done.

In the same way, tension always returns to our life, no matter how diligently we try to exterminate it.

When we try to escape tension, nature simply finds a way to transport us to a new level of tension.

For example, when we quit our job or marriage, we almost immediately experience the tension of finding a replacement job or marriage.

That's because we can quit a job or relationship any day of the week; but we can't *find* a replacement job or relationship every day of the week.

Then, when we ultimately find a new job — or a new marriage — it's a matter of time before we're back full circle with the same tension … the same compelling urge to simply quit and get *more*.

Even if we happen to find the ideal job or ideal situation or ideal mate, the tension inevitably returns.

That's because once we capture our ideal, it has a tendency to fly away and become ephemeral again. So, now we have to devote an inordinate amount of energy to make sure we hang on to it.

This is compounded by a nagging doubt *within us* that questions whether hanging on to this ideal is worth it, whether we're getting back what we're putting into it.

Before long, we start taking what we have for granted.

Without realizing it, we raise our standard for what's ideal. And so, our existing situation becomes no longer good enough.

In this way, we set ourself up for a never-ending cycle of disillusion and discontent. We wreak continuous havoc in our own life as well as in the lives of those around us.

It's a Myth:

Things
will
get
"better"

We succumb so easily to the allure of the Information Age because there's a tangible tension between what we want and what we need.

Most of us are unable to distinguish what we want from what we need.

For example, we all want an attractive, youthful life partner. But what we really *need* is a partner who will love us and stand by our side for life.

We want to eat what our taste buds demand. But what we really *need* is what is good and nutritious for our bodies.

We all want consistency and security. But what we really *need* is growth and improvement … both of which are incompatible with consistency and security.

We all want to reduce our pain, our fears, our sufferings. But what we don't realize is that we *need* pain.

We need pain because it's motivating. We learn more about ourselves during 10 days of adversity than we learn during 10 months of pleasure. We grow. We become better human beings.

We all want freedom … freedom of speech, freedom from our parents, freedom from government and bureaucracy. But what we really *need* is self-discipline.

Without self-discipline, we can never sustain the freedom we seek.

We all want a promotion at work. We all want to be top dog. We all want to run a million-dollar empire.

But what we really *need* is to do something that we're really good at so that it brings us everlasting and *innate* satisfaction.

So many people set up lofty goals for themselves. Then, they struggle to achieve these goals. But, when they finally capture it, they become miserable. Because it is not *who they are;* it's not what brings them deep satisfaction.

For example, an engineer might strive to become the Engineering Manager. But if his sense of fulfillment comes from creating and innovating, he'll never be happy as a manager. A manager has to love to lead, administrate, organize, coach. He also has to take in his stride all the politicking, negotiating, and networking that come with the territory.

We think we want data from computers. But what we really *need* is that data "massaged" and overlayed with interpretation and opinion of how to best use it. Since most companies can only see what they *want* from computers, they drown in reams of useless paper, reports and spreadsheets.

With new systems, we want the perfect, show-case system with every bell and whistle. But what we really *need* is an effective system that will help us produce perfect, show-case products and provide perfect, show-case service.

Once again, most executives are so enamored with the glory of their state-of-the-art systems, they end up with embarrassing white elephants.

We want things to *look* impressive. What we need are things that *perform* impressively.

For example, most of the best-run factories don't look impressive at all. In contrast, most of the worst-run factories are lined with the latest machining technologies.

With the Wisdom of Ecology, you see *both* your wants and your needs. You see what drives you and also see what actualizes you.

And you clearly see the consequences of selecting either path. So, whichever path you choose, you are never surprised or disappointed with the outcome.

The Wisdom of Ecology doesn't mean that you squelch your ambitions, your goals, your desires.

It simply means that your ambitions get cast in their true light.

When your Wisdom of Ecology is the foundation of your goals and dreams, your wisdom taps the energy inherent in your environment and thus, initiates the fulfillment of your dreams and desires.

That's because your dreams may be high and lofty. But they are untarnished by the fantasy ideal.

You pursue your goals, not to escape the tension, but *despite* the tension.

You are not motivated by a compulsion to run *away* from things.

You know that you can run away from your present environment. But you can never run away from yourself.

In the Information Age, we are programmed to pursue everything in our life — our relationships, our jobs, our things, even our ideas — to *own* it and accumulate it, not to appreciate it.

We are led to believe that accumulating objects and money and status and power will make us happy and tension-free.

But the reality of nature always disappoints us.

As you align your expectations with nature's inclination, you become more acutely aware that the people around you are not in touch with *their* Wisdom of Ecology.

You see the tension and turbulence that reigns on their lives.

You see that they don't truly appreciate their environment. They take the good things around them for granted. Their day-to-day needs are so powerful, they can't focus on anything but escaping their own struggle.

Sadly, they usually aren't even aware of the effect they have on other people ... including you.

When you give kindly and generously to such people, you know that it's a matter of time before these very same people will take your efforts for granted and simply expect *more* from you.

For example, as a parent, if you're compassionate and understanding, your kids will soon want more compassion from you. Worse, they might secretly wonder whether behind all that kindness, you're really a wimp.

As a partner to your mate, if you're passionate and affectionate, your partner will soon be bored to the point of wanting variations of that passion ... or worse, your partner will soon feel suffocated, and yearn for some time and space away from you.

It is the *necessity* of nature that even when you *know* inside that you've become a better person, that you're doing a better job, that you've become more caring and considerate than ever before, that your environment gives you feedback that you're *not* doing "okay" anymore.

But with your Wisdom of Ecology, you don't get disgruntled or disillusioned by the seeming lack of gratitude around you.

You rely on the wisdom of your convictions — not the feedback around you — to give you the impetus to forge forward.

In the business world, many crises have their root in the simple fact that our employees, our customers and our co-workers don't have their Wisdom of Ecology awakened.

And so, their expectations race ahead of our capabilities.

For example, as a boss, if you grant Fridays as casual-dress days, your employees will soon start demanding that *all* days be casual-dress days. If you switch to a four-day work-week flexible schedule, it will be a matter of time before your employees feel *entitled* to this flexibility, rather than feeling grateful for the privilege.

If you take care of all the fundamental needs of all your employees — such as clean restrooms, well-lit work spaces — it will be a matter of time before your employees feel frustrated because they don't hear enough about what's going in the organization.

Take care of that problem and it will be a matter of time before they want to participate in decision-making.

As an employee, if you establish a track record of reliability and dependability, you'll find your boss tending towards assigning you the bigger and more demanding tasks, thus perhaps stretching you beyond your capabilities.

As a business, if you offer your customers 24-hour turnaround, it will be a matter of time before your customers take this for granted and start demanding even faster service.

If your *competitor* offers 24-hour turnaround — and you don't — it will be a matter of time before your customers will *assume* that you offer it too. And *then,* they will start demanding faster service.

In the automotive industry, what used to be considered high quality barely a decade ago is unacceptable today.

And optional luxuries like a cup holder quickly became necessary standard equipment.

When you live in the Wisdom of Ecology, you see all these events before they happen. And so, you're equipped and energized to dissolve them, while others are still playing catch-up.

Most people expect that, once they solve a problem, they can lay that problem to rest, and then move on to solve other problems.

With the Wisdom of Ecology, you know that nature abhors a tension-free environment.

And so, you fully expect that every problem you solve will inevitably lead to a new problem.

And that more often than not, this new problem will be a bigger, more insidious, version of the very problem you intended to solve.

For example, office computers were intended to improve productivity and also, to solve the problem of too much paper.

But productivity gains have yet to materialize. That's because the time saved from using computers is often offset by the inordinate time required to keep them running, install frequent software upgrades, wade through phone-book-size manuals and decipher intimidating, unnecessary bells and whistles.

And paper usage, instead of shrinking, has skyrocketed. That's because we are seduced by the computer's speed and so, we create more reports, more paper, more analysis. We don't have time to read such analyses. But we inevitably have to find the time to sift, file, categorize — and ultimately, shred — these new charts and reports.

In a similar fashion, e-mail, voice mail, fax and cellular phones were designed to make our lives more efficient and more organized. But communication has been speeded up and systematized so well that the *volume* of communication has skyrocketed, thus throwing our lives into even greater disarray.

The many options for communication have been both a blessing ... and a curse.

In the Information Age, we are on a constant quest to ease the tensions in our life through the use of innovation, machines and technologies.

But nature is always one step ahead of us, racing to replace our old tensions with new tensions.

Refrigerators were designed to reduce food waste by keeping our perishable foods fresh. But because we can store our perishables, we tend to buy more food than we need. Which actually results in more food waste because the food spoils before we can consume it, and, some might say, also because we tend to overeat.

Water filters were designed to remove contaminants from tap water. But, if we fail to replace the filter according to a precise schedule, the water that comes through the filtering device can actually be *dirtier* than it was before.

Automatic numerically-controlled machines were designed to minimize operator error. They've done this well. But we now have to contend with *programmer* errors which can be far more costly.

We also have the cost and hassle of a rigorous maintenance schedule that tolerates no slack.

The deregulation of telecommunications and the break-up of AT&T was designed to increase competition, and lower prices. But it has resulted in so many choices and so much confusion that most of us can't tell what the lowest price is.

We've all strived hard for freedom of speech. But one of the undesirable consequences of this crusade has been freedom of speech for pornographers through magazines, videos and the internet.

Another result of freedom of speech is the increase in sex and violence on TV and in the movies. Each season brings a new high in explicitness and gore. That's because the audience learns to accept the new level, gets filled with a sense of "been there, done that," and refuses to pay for any production that doesn't go beyond the previous high.

As a nation, we aren't willing to give up the right to own handguns. But as a result, we're gradually elevating handguns from an instrument to be revered to something as ubiquitous as telephones, computers and VCR's. We're gradually changing our society from one of warmth and security to one founded on fear and insecurity.

With the Wisdom of Ecology, you gain an unusual insight into what the future holds for you … and the people around you.

You know that no matter how thoughtfully you plan things out, nature will have its way.

Expectations and standards will be raised continuously.

Each solution will lead to a new problem.

Yesterday's breakthrough will become today's entitlement.

Today's discovery will become tomorrow's price of entry.

The Wisdom of Ecology does *not* mean that we stop trying to make things "better."

It does *not* mean that we should learn to cope with our present environment no matter how high the tension gets.

It does *not* mean that we give up on improvements and innovations and technology.

A gardener doesn't stop weeding just because he knows that the job of weeding never ends.

But it is a wise gardener who harnesses the power of nature.

Most people design their landscape and choose their plantings based on the latest craze, or on what's most pleasing to the eye.

The wise gardener pays attention to the forces of nature. He picks species that are native to the area, or adaptive to the area. He even creatively uses plants others might discard as pestilent weeds.

When you have foreknowledge, rather being just a pawn in the game of life, you become the master.

Rather than falling behind the curve, you get ahead of the curve.

You don't wait for others to raise the standards. You *set* the higher standard. And even as you're setting the latest standard, you prepare to be the one to introduce the *next* higher standard.

For example, when Sony introduced the Walkman, it knew it had a huge hit on its hands. But Sony also saw the inevitable competition from "me-too" competitors. Rather than wait for the competitors to change the rules of the game, Sony changed the rules *itself*. Even as it introduced the first-generation models of Walkmans, it was readying to release the *next-*generation models.

Because of this simple wisdom, the Sony Walkman still remains the leader, despite its many imitators.

In contrast, when Hughes (a division of General Motors) introduced DirecTV a satellite broadcasting alternative to cable TV, it lacked the wisdom to see the inevitable competition. So, DirecTV soared impressively for a year. Then, it succumbed to "me-too" competitors that undercut its price by 75%.

With the Wisdom of Ecology, you don't wait for the next problem to erupt as a result of the latest solution. You define the problem and prepare to offer its solution.

Knowing *which* standard to set or *which* new problem to solve comes through the Wisdom of Aggregation.

Ecology lays the groundwork for Aggregation.

Combined, Ecology and Aggregation become the wellspring of good fortune for you.

Most people are driven by their search for security. Everything they do — the education they get, the careers they choose, the relationships they create — is motivated by a need for security and stability.

They never realize that the kind of stability they seek is nowhere to be found.

In nature, nothing is stable. Nothing remains still.

Everything is constantly moving, changing, evolving.

The earth is constantly revolving on its axis.

It is also constantly rotating around the sun.

And it is the *tension* between the earth and the sun that keeps the earth from hurling aimlessly and dangerously into space.

The stability of the earth is *created* by its instability.

Its security comes from the *rhythm* of its insecurity.

With the Wisdom of Ecology, you know that the only thing that remains stable is instability, the only thing that remains unchanged is the force of constant change.

So, like a surfer, you don't resist the wave of change. Instead, you aim to ride the crest of change.

You don't brace yourself, wondering whether you'll be swallowed up by the uncertain future.

You go out and *create* the future.

The quality of your life, instead of being soaked with fear, gets showered with enthusiasm for the promise of the future.

Amazingly, as you embrace insecurity, you inevitably secure your future.

Because, as others recognize that you are the architect of change — the beacon for the future — they instinctively turn to you for direction and leadership.

A surfer doesn't shirk huge waves. Instead, he welcomes them — even seeks them out — because he knows that they offer the best surfing opportunities.

Similarly, you don't dread periods of tension and chaos. Instead, you welcome them — even seek them out — because you know they offer the best opportunities for success, growth and accomplishment.

Accessing
THE WISDOM OF ECOLOGY

(1)   Today, I will look at all the changes I'm striving to make in my life. Am I being honest with myself about my motivations? If I am merely attempting to escape from my present discomforts, do I recognize that this is an empty goal? If I'm indeed aspiring to a higher plateau, have I mentally accepted that this new plateau will bring with it new levels of tension?

(2)   Today, I will remind myself to appreciate and acknowledge everything I have, in all its detail, and despite the tension.

(3)   Do I anticipate the tension that comes as a result of all progress? By my actions and decisions, do I lead the pack ... or am I a mere follower, always playing catch-up?

The Wisdom

of

Aggregation

The universe appears to be
vast, complex, and overwhelming.
Yet, everything follows a predictable pattern,
eagerly waiting to be be uncovered.

And once you see these patterns,
your life enters a new stage,
brimming with success and good fortune.

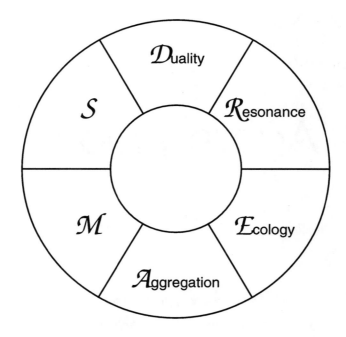

Nothing is more terrible
than activity
without insight.

Thomas Carlyle

With the Wisdoms of Duality, Resonance and Ecology, you've become able to see the paradoxes and the ambiguities and the tensions that are intrinsic to nature … and to your life.

The Wisdom of Aggregation is your next step up.

With the Wisdom of Aggregation, you get elevated to a higher perspective.

The word *Aggregate* means a mass of distinct things gathered into a whole.

And when you see the world around you as one big interconnected, interrelated whole, you begin to see what otherwise appears invisible, you comprehend what otherwise appears incomprehensible, you discern *patterns* that otherwise appear impenetrable.

Every distinct entity in the universe, from the tiniest cell to the largest planet, appears at first glance to be chaotic, random, intricate.

But when you move to a higher perspective, so you can see everything in aggregate, an exquisite and vibrant mosaic emerges.

And once you see this mosaic, you see the harmony behind the chaos. You discern the predictability behind the uncertainty. You hear the symphony behind the chatter and the flutter.

The experience is similar to that of gazing out of the window of a plane as it is taking off.

At first, when you're still at ground level, you notice only a few buildings, only a few planes, only a handful of people.

As your plane soars up into the sky, you start seeing buildings you couldn't see before. You begin to see roads and routes you didn't know existed. You see how all these roads are networked and interconnected. And you see how these roads can take you to places you couldn't imagine existed before.

Over the years, we've all been taught to look at the world around us from "ground level."

This is why we're unable to see the quick, sure shortcuts around our obstacles, even though these shortcuts are always available to us.

And this is why we miss the tremendously rich opportunities, even though these opportunities are always within our reach.

With the higher perspective of your Wisdom of Aggregation, you quickly pinpoint these life-saving shortcuts. You home in directly on to these joyous opportunities.

That's because you look at the pieces of the puzzle in aggregate. And so you are able to see how these pieces fit together.

In this way, you make the most effective decisions. You pick the optimum actions. And accomplishing your goals becomes inevitable.

The symbol of the Wisdom of Aggregation is the eagle.

Just as the eagle soars high above everything and scans the entire landscape, with the Wisdom of Aggregation, you soar high and easily see the big picture.

You quickly put the people, things and events in their larger context.

You see the world as it really is.

You see what's really going on.

So, you focus your energies where it really makes a difference.

There are seven facets of awakening your Wisdom of Aggregation. Each facet is remarkably straightforward. Each facet serves to progressively elevate your perspective.

The first facet of awakening your Wisdom of Aggregation involves opening our eyes.

In the Information Age, most of us are overwhelmed by the flood of information being unleashed on us. So, we deliberately block out most of the information streaming towards us unless we can immediately see the relevance of that information.

But the relief we get from closing our eyes is only temporary.

Because the long-term effect is that it hinders our ability to see the *patterns* that govern our lives.

Our perspective gets limited.

And this limited perspective conceals the vast sea of options from us.

We become unable to see all our options.

We become unable to see our *best* options. We aren't even aware that these optimum options *exist.*

So, we are quick to jump on the first option that comes our way. And in this way, we easily settle for second best.

With the Wisdom of Aggregation, you open your eyes to the infinite details around you.

But you don't look *at* the details. You look *for* the patterns.

You're not interested in the details. You're interested in how the details are *connected.*

Rather than being overwhelmed, you feel exhilarated.

You become able to see a vast array of options. You see options that remain invisible to most others.

You see your way through the maze of life while others are still oblivious to the fact that they're in a maze.

The second facet of awakening your Wisdom of Aggregation involves looking beyond what's immediately obvious.

For example, when most of us look at the night sky, we see just a cluster of stars, scattered randomly from horizon to horizon.

But when you look beyond what's immediately obvious, you see that certain stars are always in the same formation relative to other stars.

Each of us may interpret these formations differently. For example, the stars that are the basis of the astrological sign of Sagittarius appear as a horse-rider to some and as a teapot to others.

But members of both groups have an edge over those who don't see the formation at all. Because those who see the formation can use it to navigate themselves when they're lost. While those who don't see the formation at all will stumble for a long time in the dark.

The Dilbert comic strip has succeeded so tremendously because Scott Adams, its creator, looked beyond what's immediately obvious.

Most comic strips focus on children, animals and outlandish characters. And because this is what's immediately obvious, almost every aspiring cartoonist tries to create more of these same characters.

But Adams saw beyond the obvious. He saw that the *situation* in most offices are outlandish in themselves. He saw that all of us find our bosses frustrating and ultimately laughable.

And so he created a cartoon strip that focuses on the very real antics and tactics of bosses and co-workers. Because he looked beyond what's immediately obvious, Adams was able to create the fastest-growing comic strip in the history of newspaper publishing.

When we see only what's immediately obvious, we almost always see the obstacles and barriers that prevent us from moving forward.

But when you look beyond what's immediately obvious, the impossible becomes possible.

That's because the obstacles we first perceive are really only opportunities in disguise.

It's a Myth:

Live
in the
here
and now

The third facet of awakening your Wisdom of Aggregation involves looking across the artificial boundaries of time.

We've all been besieged to live in the here and the now.

Spiritual gurus and self-help authors implore us to live in the present ... forget about the past ... let the future take care of itself ... simply, live for the moment.

As you will see with the Wisdom of Stratification, it is important to make every moment full and worthwhile.

But it is also important to *look* at the past, present and the future.

With your Wisdom of Aggregation, you look for the *patterns* in the pastiche of your past, your present and your future.

You relish the present. But you're always grateful for the people and events that brought you to your present. You're always grateful for the lessons and experiences of your past. And you also look to the promise of the future ... for yourself *and* for the people around you.

Because you have a long-term (past, present and future) view of your life, day-to-day events have little bearing on your moods. Short-term up's or down's have little effect on your actions or your choices. Today's headlines and today's fads leave you unperturbed.

You look out at the ocean of life, towards the horizon with all its potentials and all its possibilities. While most people can see only the erratic waves breaking against the shore and get deeply disturbed.

Most people revolve into and out of friendships and relationships. You remain steadfast in your devotion to the people in your life, never forgetting what brought you together in the first place, never losing sight of the potential for your future together.

Most executives jump in and out of the latest management fads. You persevere with your projects and tasks, deviating only when the patterns change substantially.

Most people panic when the stock market dips. And they jubilate when it reaches a new high. You remain unfazed and confident of your overall direction.

The fourth facet of awakening your Wisdom of Aggregation involves looking beyond your immediate circle of friends and associates.

Most people limit their friendships and associations to those who hold similar interests, ideas and values. They circulate primarily among their immediate circle of family, peers, co-workers, church and club members.

With the Wisdom of Duality, you already know to expand your circle to include mavericks, naysayers, and devil's advocates.

Now with the Wisdom of Aggregation, you break the boundaries to include people from other clubs, other clans, other companies, other industries, other technologies, other countries, other philosophies, other religions, other functions, other hierarchies.

You expose yourself to this array of diverse experiences so that you can observe and interpret.

But you don't get overwhelmed by this vast exposure. Because your purpose is to see clearly and limitlessly, not to clog your mind.

The experience is similar to driving a car. Your focus is clearly on the road ahead. But through your peripheral vision and a series of rear-view and side-view mirrors, you are always aware of unexpected changes and random shifts that affect you.

People who limit themselves to their immediate circle of friends and associates and experiences drive on the road of life with blinders.

They don't see the quick opportunities for shortcuts until it's too late.

Worse, they don't see the magnitude of the danger about to strike them until the danger is right upon them.

By going out of your immediate circle — whether your home, your office or your board room — you become able to discern independent trends, converging trends, diverging trends.

You become able to see which new things will replace which old things.

You become able to see new ways of *combining* old things.

You become able to see new ways of using old things.

At the bottom line, you become able to see the hidden patterns that lead to unusual prosperity for you.

This fourth facet of looking beyond your immediate circle is so important because it makes it possible for you to see things you wouldn't otherwise see.

Our ability to see is limited by what we've seen before.

For example, if we weren't familiar with the colors red and blue, we'd have difficulty discerning the composite of these two colors, which is purple.

On the other hand, once we know how to distinguish red and blue, we become able to quickly discern the color purple ... as well as its various hues and shades, such as lavender and mauve.

In other words, the more we see, the more we become able to see.

When the original Starbucks opened in Seattle, the founder couldn't see beyond his immediate neighborhood. He was happy to sell rich flavors of coffee in large variety to the local community.

But an employee of Starbucks, Howard Schultz, on a business trip to Italy, noticed the 200,000 espresso bars throughout Italy ... and he saw the power of replicating the Starbucks concept McDonald's-style across the nation and across the planet. So, he bought out the Starbucks company, became its CEO and Chairman, and took an old commodity like coffee to create an entirely new industry.

Most people *wait* for fortune to shine on them. That's because they're blind to the fortune that already lies in front of them.

With the Wisdom of Aggregation, you see a world full of possibilities ahead of you. By seeing in aggregate, by looking outside your comfort zone, and then by discerning the patterns, you *cause* serendipity to happen in your life.

Most people think you need a high I.Q. to spot the emerging trends.

With the Wisdom of Aggregation, you know that you can spot trends — and also, *start* them — simply by seeing what's working tremendously in one industry, or one country and applying it to another industry or another country.

Most people think you need to be unusually creative and innovative to gain an edge in today's world.

With the Wisdom of Aggregation, you know that you just need to see across all boundaries and across time. You know that most breakthroughs are really minor variations of what's *already* working *somewhere else.* You know that the future is merely a special case of the past.

For example, the TV show, "America's Funniest Home Videos," is merely an Americanized version of an already tremendously popular show in Japan.

Sam Walton, of Wal-Mart fame, designed his discount warehouse-style store, Sam's Place, as a mid-Western copycat version of the tremendously successful pioneer of warehouse stores, San Diego-based Price Club. (Price Club since merged with Costco).

With the Wisdom of Aggregation, your "luck" depends on what and how you *see.*

The fifth facet of awakening your Wisdom of Aggregation involves looking for *what's* going on and not letting it get clouded by your need to understand *why* it's going on.

Most people have an overpowering desire to analyze things, to understand them, and to rationalize them.

So, they devote an inordinate amount of time trying to decipher *why things are the way they are.*

At home, when a lover is feuding, we struggle to understand *why.*

At work, when a process doesn't work in a particular way, we put teams together to analyze *why.*

When one marketing campaign succeeds over another, we rationalize the possible reasons *why.*

And in our search for the answer to the question *why,* we collect even more data, even more information, thinking that somehow the additional information will shed more light.

But we always reach a point where *extra* information only serves to cloud our vision and confuse us and thus, reduce our ability to see *what's* going on.

We get so tangled in this need to analyze and understand and control, we fail to take the time to interpret *what's working.*

The sixth facet of awakening your Wisdom of Aggregation involves observing the behavior of the people who effect your future.

In the Information Age, we are so enamored with gathering data and information that we pay far too much attention to what people say and not enough to what they *do.*

For example, market researchers ardently collect people's opinions. They overlook the fact that people often say one thing and do another.

With the Wisdom of Aggregation, your emphasis is not on collecting data, but on observing it and interpreting it.

You pay attention to people's *actions* … rather than their opinions or their memories or their promises.

Most people feel frustrated and betrayed when the people around them fail to do what they said they would do.

But because you observe and interpret, you're rarely surprised. You merely nod knowingly and wisely as people do what their past actions indicated they would do.

When the Coca-Cola company was contemplating introducing a new formula, which they called New Coke, they conducted extensive market research. And the people who participated in their research told them that they overwhelmingly preferred the new formula to the classic formula.

But, in the marketplace, *in the real world,* new Coke failed miserably. *The public didn't do what they said they would do.*

And so, Coca-Cola had to bring back the old formula under the name, Classic Coke.

Coca-Cola could have saved itself the embarrassment and the expense by paying attention up front to how people *behaved.*

In the Information Age, we have a tendency to mistake data for wisdom. Fortunately, a few people have had the wisdom to act, not on data, but on what they see about human behavior.

For example, had the people who pioneered the automobile, the personal computer, the telephone, and the answering machine based their actions on market data, they would have given up very early in the game.

Market data said that consumers didn't want automobiles. Market data said that people couldn't see a practical use for personal computers.

Yet, Henry Ford persisted. So did Steve Jobs.

That's because they could both see the *fundamental human needs* their devices fulfilled.

They could see that it was inevitable that consumers would embrace their devices and use them as *extensions* of themselves.

It was a wisdom developed through observing the behavior of humans.

This sixth facet of looking at the behavior of people is so important because you can use it to predict your future — and even *create* it.

There's one key variable that weaves through practically every pattern in nature.

And that key variable is human behavior.

Human behavior governs the pace and the quality of nearly every outcome.

For example, technology may move forward at breakneck speed. But ultimately, the pace at which technology will become useful in the real world will be governed by human acceptance of that technology.

This is what has happened with computers.

Computers have the potential to instantly revolutionize how we communicate.

But this potential is being realized in stages. Because humans have an inborn resistance to change. Also, they have a limited ability to absorb new concepts.

This overarching pattern of human behavior affects nearly everything that happens around you.

And remarkably, this pattern is very *predictable.*

That's because most humans don't radically change how they react to specific situations.

This is why once you see these patterns — and as long as you also see the people around you through your Wisdoms of Duality, Magnanimity and Stratification — you can create any future for yourself that you desire.

The seventh facet of awakening your Wisdom of Aggregation involves seeing the world and *accepting* it as non-linear.

In the Information Age, we are obsessed with getting linear answers to everything.

For example, most business owners and managers place their focus on the *bottom line.*

But a business is far more than just the bottom line.

Nothing can be reduced to a single measurement or calculation.

To create true success for a business, we must remove our "linear" blinders and see the people, the customers, the competitors, the processes, the history, and the future, among other things.

In addition, we must look at characteristics like the quality, the cycle time, the customer perception, the competitions' perceptions.

We must look for the patterns that connect these aspects of our business in aggregate.

Unfortunately, we prefer to act like one of the six blind men in the famous children's story.

These blind men have never seen an elephant before. So, when, the first blind man feels the trunk of the elephant, he thinks it's a snake in front of him. When the second blind man feels the huge leg of the elephant, he thinks it's a tree trunk in front of him. And so on.

With the Wisdom of Aggregation, you finally remove your blinders and experience the elephant the way it was meant to be experienced ... in three-dimension, and in aggregate.

This seventh facet of seeing and *accepting* the world as nonlinear is important because it allows you to move quickly forward.

In the Information Age, most people struggle to devise the perfect solution to every problem.

But in a non-linear world with so many variables, more often than not, partially perfect solutions are the most effective.

For example, many companies design their forms and paperwork to take care of every possible situation. Thus, they make their forms and systems cumbersome for everyone.

With the Wisdom of Aggregation, you see that designing your forms and paper systems to handle the most common situations frees you up to handle the occasional out-of-ordinary requirements.

Similarly, many companies establish rigid rules to monitor and control their employees.

With the Wisdom of Aggregation, you see that most employees are not out to cheat your company. And so, you become willing to introduce flexibility into your work schedule, even though it creates a small exposure to abuse.

Similarly, when designing a customer service guarantee, most companies get concerned that if their guarantee is too liberal and too slanted in the customers' favor, they would become the target of rip-off artists.

With the Wisdom of Aggregation, you see that most people are honorable. And so, a liberal guarantee that gives peace of mind to the vast majority of your customers is well worth the small risk you assume.

In the Information Age, we expend energy where our efforts are quickly dissipated.

That's because we erect barriers that prevent us from seeing what's really going on.

As we wrestle and dodge these self-imposed barriers, we get easily frustrated with the people and events in our lives.

With the Wisdom of Aggregation, you quickly put things in their proper perspective.

Seeing things in their proper perspective is very liberating. Because it frees you to tackle the *real* obstacles in your life.

On the following pages are examples of barriers we erect in front of ourselves and how the Wisdom of Aggregation frees us from these barriers so that we may lead fruitful, joyous lives.

The patterns on the following pages provide only a framework. Since we live in a non-linear world, you should use these frameworks only as a starting point to seeing the patterns that create the world around you.

As a marriage or relationship progresses, most people get increasingly frustrated as they uncover more and more differences between their partner and themselves.

But with the Wisdom of Aggregation, you know this is the *natural pattern* of getting to know another person. It is rare that two people share the exact same combination of habits, idiosyncrasies, likes and dislikes.

With your wisdom, you *expect* these differences to manifest themselves as time progresses. You *see* them coming. You *expect* sexual desire to wane as the years progress.

And so, you focus on building intimacy and trust, rather than on the growing, day-to-day, inconsequential differences.

Most people don't see the changes coming. So, they get immersed in frustration, blaming and self-doubt. This undermines the relationship and ultimately breaks it up.

When differences first develop, most people create a physical and emotional distance between themselves. They break off communications. Or they engage in a volley of blame and counter-blame. Molehills become mountains, thus leading to inevitable explosion.

With the Wisdom of Aggregation, you are aware of these patterns of human behavior. So, rather than allowing emotions to rule, you take responsibility for the *predictable* results of your behavior.

You recognize that the longer things are allowed to fester, the more difficult it will be to repair the damage.

So, you move swiftly one-on-one, face-to-face to put matters to bed, and head-off any acrimonious confrontations.

Most therapists claim that, when a marriage is on the rocks, it is indicative of long-repressed, fundamental problems in the marriage.

But, with the Wisdoms of Ecology and Aggregation, you see the tensions inevitable in *every* marriage.

As each partner's individual needs are met by the marriage, he/she raises his/her expectations. What was good yesterday is no longer good today. If the partner was a good communicator yesterday, then that partner must be a good communicator *and* an expert at creating intimacy today.

Ironically, the *better* the marriage, the *more* tenuous it becomes.

Once again, because you see the inevitable patterns, you focus your gaze on your common goals and values.

On the job, many people complain that they have the responsibility to complete an assignment; but they don't have the authority.

With the Wisdom of Aggregation, you see the situation in its true context. You recognize that, in fact, *no one* has both the responsibility and the authority ... not even the top person on the totem pole.

For instance, the top person has the responsibility to get customers to buy the company's products. But the top person can *never* have any authority over the customers.

With the Wisdom of Aggregation, you also recognize that the power you get as a result of a title is ultimately useless, even counter-productive. The only power you can have over other people is the one *they* vest in you because you *earn* it from *them*.

So, you stop expending your energies on convincing your higher-ups to give you more power. Instead, you focus your efforts on fulfilling your responsibilities and earning the trust and respect of those you have to lead.

The Wisdom of Aggregation reveals that all change goes through a cycle of initial hoopla; followed by frustration because the actual progress doesn't keep pace with the hoopla; followed by a gradual assimilation into the mainstream, usually noticeable only in hindsight.

The initial hoopla phase usually involves people introducing unnecessary bells and whistles. That's because, during this phase, everyone tries to distinguish himself by the number and type of features he offers.

The assimilation period usually involves a long-drawn-out restructuring and reorganizing and redesigning as everyone adjusts to the new way of things. This is the period where emphasis moves towards making things truly efficient.

This is what happened with the introduction of the personal computer.

Actually, the same pattern occurred on both the users' side as well as the sellers' side.

On the computer users' side, during the initial hoopla, a lot of people raced to buy computers.

Then, everyone became frustrated because the computers didn't live up to their promise and so, computers became the proverbial door stop.

This was followed by a long period where people slowly but surely redesigned how they worked to take advantage of the new powers of the computer.

On the sales side of personal computers, the initial hoopla period involved a lot of extraneous bells and whistles, as each computer manufacturer vied for consumer attention.

Then, as consumers realized that neither the speed nor the features were paying off, computer sales plummeted.

This was followed by a streamlining of computer manufacturing, which brought prices down and made computers accessible and necessary in every home and office.

97

Most people place their emphasis on creativity when it comes to advertising and marketing.

But the Wisdom of Aggregation reveals two distinct patterns of human behavior that effect the success of your advertising.

The first pattern of human behavior that effects the success of your advertising is the awareness level of your consumers about your product or service.

If you are first with a product or service, your advertising can be plain and direct. All you have to do is address the consumer's need and how you can fulfill it.

If you are second with a product, you have to show how you can fulfill the consumer's need better than the competition.

If you have many competitors, you can't outshout your competitors any more. The consumer is overwhelmed, and has difficulty differentiating between competing brands. Perhaps the consumer has tried some of your competitor's products. The only way to stand out is to show how you can fulfill the consumer's need in a *new* way, using a new process.

If the market is saturated with competitors, your advertising has to move beyond features, beyond price, beyond quality, beyond new processes. That's because the consumer is hardened and skeptical of the claims and counter-claims. So, your advertising has to entertain. It has to be loaded with valuable information the consumer can use at once. Most importantly, it has to bond with your consumer, where you acknowledge his savvy *and* his skepticism.

The second distinct pattern of human behavior that affects the success of your advertising is the behavior of your competition.

Most people bury their head in the sand and pretend that the competition doesn't exist.

With the Wisdom of Aggregation, you expand your circle of vision. You know that your competitors are not only those who sell the same product as you do; they are also others from whom your customers might buy other products as an alternate to your product.

For example, Southwest Airlines sees clearly that its competitors are not just other airlines, but buses and personal automobiles as well. The consumer can choose to drive as an alternate to flying. So, Southwest Airlines prices its flights to compete with the cost of driving.

With the Wisdom of Aggregation, you know that every move you make is subject to a counter-move by your competitor.

Every time you cut prices, your competitor can match or beat your lower price.

Plus, your consumer now *expects* this lower price from you. If your price cut was temporary, the consumer *waits* until the next time you temporarily cut prices again.

Every time you offer rebates, you can be sure your competition will soon follow on your heels.

With the Wisdom of Aggregation, you know to look for patterns that set you completely apart from your competition.

The Wisdom of Aggregation gives you a unique edge.

Because of your broad perspective, you are able to clearly see your own strengths and weaknesses.

You are also able to clearly see the strengths and weaknesses of your competition.

The Wisdom of Duality gives you the ability to see these strengths and weaknesses without self-recrimination, without judgement, without ego.

And so, you're able to see how you can combine your own strengths with your competitor's weaknesses to gain a substantial edge for yourself.

For example, Southwest Airlines saw that the major airlines were saddled with huge overheads. They saw the stuffy, bureaucratic environment of their competitors. And they saw how these very weaknesses could become their own strengths. They saw how they could fashion a low-overhead, fun airline that would spontaneously draw customers.

Wal-Mart saw how all the major department stores were focusing their attention entirely in the major metropolitan areas, leaving the small towns and rural communities unattended. They saw how this weakness in their competition could be fashioned into their own strength.

Blockbuster Videos saw that mom-and-pop video stores were doomed from the start. So, instead of settling for a small, local chain of video stores, they set out to create a nationwide chain that rented a larger, more diverse collection of videos than any store in each neighborhood.

FedEx saw the bureaucracy that riddled the U. S. Postal Service. They saw how this bureaucracy created a weakness in that letters and packages always took much longer to deliver than the consumer needed.

These opportunities had always existed in plain sight for anyone to see. But only Herb Kelleher, Sam Walton, Wayne Huzienga and Fred Smith, respectively, were in touch with their Wisdom of Aggregation to see the patterns.

Most people play the blame game. They blame their lack of success on their limited resources. They blame it on the huge advantages that established companies have. They blame it on the deep discounts that larger companies get.

When the blame game doesn't work, such people move on to the protect-me game. They seek protection from the "big guys." They seek subsidies. They seek tariffs.

With the Wisdom of Aggregation, you know that the blame game and the protect-me game are only temporary stop-gaps.

So, you open your eyes and look for the abundant opportunities in front of you to create your own niche.

Southwest Airlines and Wal-Mart are both examples of small companies that refused to play the blame game and the protect-me game. Both companies emerged from nowhere and captured prominent success spontaneously ... simply because they were willing to see things differently.

Enterprise Rent-A-Car is another company that refused to play the blame game. Most car rental companies position themselves at expensive locations next to airports. Only Enterprise saw the pattern that people who turn in their cars at auto service stations need a rental car to get to and from work.

So, Enterprise located itself at cheap locations next to auto service stations and created a unique niche for itself.

While all the other car rental companies were battling among themselves at the airport, progressively undercutting each other, Enterprise quietly became one of the largest car rental companies.

Enterprise Rent-A-Car is just one example of a company that steered clear off the me-too track.

Even though it was in a crowded field such as car rentals, it looked for a pattern that would make it the natural and only choice of its customers.

Many companies have found a way to enter a lucrative field that's over-crowded by deliberately rising above the crowd.

The patterns are strikingly similar.

For example, TV Guide is in the lucrative television industry. Yet, it doesn't compete directly with any of the networks or cable channels. That's because it *integrates* these channels into a weekly viewing guide.

Similarly, J.D. Power & Associates is in the lucrative automotive indus-try. Once again, it doesn't compete with any of the automotive giants because it *integrates* them through customer surveys.

Similarly, Zagat Surveys is in the restaurant industry. It *integrates* rat-ings of restaurants through its various city restaurant guides.

At the bottom line, with the Wisdom of Aggregation, it doesn't matter whether you're starting on the ground floor ... or getting into a crowded field. You look for the patterns that govern whatever field you decide to enter, and you find the one pattern that will give you a significant edge over anyone who is or plans to become your competitor.

Most businesses focus on marketing their product or service or brand name. In a look-alike, feel-alike world of business clones, such companies typically have nothing to set them apart from their competitors. So, they flounder.

With the Wisdom of Aggregation, you see that a very critical element that can set you apart from your competition is your expertise ... and your eagerness to share it.

For example, consumers don't want to just buy a tool at the best price. They want someone to guide them on how to select the best tool for the money. They also want someone to call in case they run into a problem when they get home.

But consumers just won't call anyone. It isn't enough to have the expertise and then, announce it. The consumer must *believe* you have the expertise. The consumer must *perceive* you as the expert.

Again, the Wisdom of Aggregation sheds light on how to create a *perception* of expertise.

It reveals that a small action — limiting what you do — brings big paybacks.

For example, PaperDirect is perceived as the expert in paper *because* it doesn't sell anything else but paper. When a consumer needs paper, he is much more likely to turn to PaperDirect than to a general office supply store such as Quill, or Reliable or Viking.

Focusing on one competence and doing it very well is what helps set PaperDirect apart.

Most people operate under the assumption that they have to make trade-offs whenever they have two or more needs.

For example, many companies believe that they can't provide extremely low cycle times and still maintain leadership in price. They believe that something has to give.

With the Wisdom of Aggregation, you have a different perspective. Rather than looking for tradeoffs between your needs, you look for the *relationships* between your needs.

For example, with the Wisdom of Aggregation, you see that cycle time and cost have a direct relationship ... that it is *inevitable* that you'll cut costs when you set out to slash cycle time dramatically. That's because when you find a way to cut cycle time, you inevitably remove a lot of wasted otherwise-costly motions.

You get what you see.

Most companies used to believe that it's impossible to provide low costs to customers without gouging their suppliers ... or otherwise, operating on very slim margins themselves.

But Wal-Mart, ever in touch with its Wisdom of Aggregation, saw things differently. Wal-Mart saw that it could use computer technology to keep its suppliers constantly informed of changing customer demands ... and also, to keep its own inventory carrying costs to a bare minimum.

Because Wal-Mart saw what it did, it didn't make a trade-off. It made history.

Most people believe that you need money in order to make money. So, if they have little or no money, they believe that they have no opportunity for personal or financial success.

With the Wisdom of Aggregation, you recognize that money is *not the only currency* for procuring goods and services. You know that time, knowledge and skills can be used just as easily in place of money.

So, you look at the *true needs* of the person who has the goods or services you want. Then, you look for ways to match these needs with your own time and talent.

In this way, you procure the goods and services you need by exchanging your time or knowledge, rather than money.

At the bottom line, with the Wisdom of Aggregation, you don't need money to make money.

At some point or the other in their life, most people have taken advantage of another person's money ... through the use of credit cards or when financing the purchase of a car or a home.

So they recognize the leveraging advantage they get when they use other people's money.

But few people recognize the *multi-layered* advantage of using other people's *resources*.

For example, Bill Gates of Microsoft saw the opportunity to put his MS-DOS operating system on every IBM-clone personal computer.

This opportunity was out there for any operating software company to see. Bill Gates was in touch with his Wisdom of Aggregation and so he saw it. Macintosh wasn't and so they missed it.

Bill Gates collected the combined marketing and financial muscle of practically every personal computer manufacturer. This muscle was strong enough to overpower the Macintosh operating system, even though, by most accounts, Macintosh was far superior to MS-DOS.

People bought MS-DOS, not because it was better, but because it was everywhere. They had little choice.

With the Wisdom of Aggregation, you know that success doesn't come from what you do. It comes from what you see.

Similarly, Intel saw the opportunity to partner with computer manufacturers to package its chips as standard and "inside" the computer. Digital Computer didn't access its Wisdom of Aggregation. So, it floundered.

With the Wisdom of Aggregation, you know that ultimately, Intel's success doesn't come just from its ability to design faster chips. It comes from its willingness to see the leveraging opportunities for its chips.

Few would disagree that Sony had the far superior video recorder when it introduced the Beta format.

But JVC saw that most movies run for a length of two hours. So, JVC designed its VHS format to accommodate the 2-hour time period, then used this simple convenience to get movie studios to release a large number of titles in the VHS format.

Sony didn't see this pattern. So, they devoted tremendous corporate resources to developing a technically superior product that ultimately languished.

Most people believe that innovating new products and new markets is the lifeblood of success.

With the Wisdom of Aggregation, you know that product and technical innovation, by themselves, are simply not enough.

For example, IBM did not pioneer computers. In fact, it was one of the late comers. Yet, it sailed far past the original pioneers.

And Diner's Club was the original inventor of credit cards. Yet, MasterCard, VISA and American Express have clearly left Diner's Club behind in the dust.

Microsoft is rarely first on the market with a new product. Yet, it's the world's largest software producer ... by a wide margin.

With the Wisdom of Aggregation, you know that what sets apart IBM, American Express, and Microsoft is something far more important than product or technical innovation.

With the Wisdom of Aggregation, you always have your eyes open for opportunities to collect maximum payback for your efforts.

While others devote their energies to designing perfect solutions and producing technically superior products, you look to see how you can leverage your resources.

You *always* look for ways to leverage your efforts through *other people's resources* so that, with this combined muscle, you can become the ten-ton gorilla who sits anywhere he pleases.

Those who don't see this first step usually end up desperately flailing their arms ... trying, but failing to get attention to their "better" products.

Most people spend a lot of time and energy trying to protect their ideas, hide their trade secrets, register their patents.

With the Wisdom of Aggregation, you see that your ideas are worth nothing unless you are able to leverage your resources and put your ideas firmly in the marketplace.

Without the Wisdom of Aggregation and a great idea, you are an also-ran like the Diner's Club.

With the Wisdom of Aggregation and *someone else's idea,* you can become a great entity like VISA.

Accessing
THE WISDOM OF AGGREGATION

(1)   Today, I will look at the choices and actions in front of me and consider … Do I have a clear and complete picture in front of me? Do I clearly see the patterns governing this picture?

(1)   Today, I will reflect on the way I see the world around me … Am I looking beyond my comfort zone … and across time boundaries? Am I looking beyond the "obvious"? Have I relinquished my need to analyze and understand? Do I accept the world as non-linear?

(3)   Today, I will reflect on the actions of the people in my world. What patterns can I detect from these actions? How can I use these patterns to shape my future?

(4)   Today, I will review whether my approach will truly bring me my goals with the least effort, time and money. Am I first pursuing the vital tasks that will bring me maximum payback? Have I looked for every opportunity to use other people's resources?

The Wisdom

of

Magnanimity

*It is nature's way to infuse
every human being's life
with instability and insecurity.*

*Merely seeing another person's
struggles and insecurities,
changes you at the most fundamental level.
It delivers you to the highest level
of personal, spiritual and material fulfillment.*

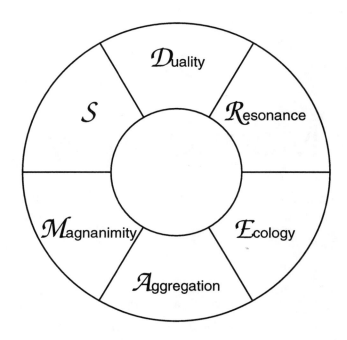

When a man has pity
on all living creatures

then only he is noble.

Buddha

With the Wisdom of Aggregation, you learned to see the world through a wide-angled lens. You learned to see everything in aggregate, across boundaries, and through multiple time zones.

With the Wisdom of Magnanimity, you learn to also see that same world through a telephoto lens, so that, in addition to seeing the events, actions and circumstances in aggregate, you can clearly see *each* of the *individuals* who dot your landscape.

With the Wisdom of Duality, you learned to see and accept the good *and* the bad in each person.

With the Wisdom of Magnanimity, you go beyond just accepting. You go beyond merely good or bad. You see the heart of the other person.

With the Wisdom of Ecology, you learned to see that tension and insecurity are the way of life.

With the Wisdom of Magnanimity, you learn to see — *benevolently* — that most people are *not* in touch with their own Wisdom of Ecology.

You learn to see that *everything* a person says or does — whether good or bad — is motivated by a feeling of insecurity and a deep-seated need to gain a feeling of security.

The cause of this insecurity may not be clear. The insecurity itself may or may not be conscious. It may not even be visible on the surface. An individual may appear on the outside to be strong and secure, perhaps egotistical, or even arrogant. An individual may be accomplished in life, or hold a position of stature.

But with the Wisdom of Magnanimity, you clearly see through the tough exterior armor. You see straight through to the insecurity inside.

You see that often those who are accomplished in life are more insecure than the rest. That's because they have farther to fall.

The symbol of the Wisdom of Magnanimity is the heart.

And with the Wisdom of Magnanimity, you learn to look at each individual in your life, not through your eyes, but through your heart.

The word Magnanimous comes from the Latin *magnus,* meaning great, and *animus,* meaning soul. The dictionary defines magnanimity as generosity, forgiveness, nobility, rising above pettiness.

And with the Wisdom of Magnanimity, you see every individual with generosity, forgiveness and nobility.

The simple act of changing how you see every person around you in a new light *changes you.*

It changes how you think of the other person.

It changes what you say to the other person.

It changes *how* you speak to the other person.

Most importantly, it causes you to stop doing things *to* the other person … and instead, start doing things *with* the other person and *for* the other person.

Waking up this wisdom inside you is actually very simple: Make the decision that every time you see another person, you will see them through your heart to the insecurity they harbor inside.

The more frequently you look for this insecurity, the more keenly you'll actually see it. This will bring you confidence in the powerful effects of this wisdom. And soon, this new way of viewing the people in your life will become ingrained in you.

This simple change of seeing the insecurity choreographs an infinity of feelings and responses in other people that lead to major personal and financial rewards for you.

But you don't change how you see others in order to collect these rewards. Because your sincerity and intention are vital.

The more sincere you are about truly seeing and understanding another person's insecurities, the greater your rewards.

Your rewards are proportionate to how genuinely you see people differently.

It is ironical that with the Wisdom of Magnanimity, the most selfish way of being is to become <u>un</u>selfish.

One of the sad ironies of the Information Age is that we have so much information around us; yet, we fail to see the patterns that reveal the reality.

For example, today more than any other time in history, we are all acutely informed about the immense suffering that commands all the lives on the planet.

The media is plastered everyday with stories of violence, abuse, addictions, terrorism, hunger, floods, hurricanes, ad infinitum.

Yet, most of us are so focused on our own problems, obstacles and insecurities, that we can't *really* see the suffering around us.

We believe that no one else has it as bad as we do.

As we are consumed with our own goals and ambitions, we become oblivious to the needs and fears of others around us.

We mentally isolate ourselves from the people around us ... even when we are surrounded by so many people.

For practical purposes, the world doesn't exist beyond us. We are the center — and the entirety — of the universe.

When we are so hobbled by our own bottom line, our own financial goals, our own possessions, we fail to *connect* with the people around us. We fail to connect with reality. We don't see that others view us as mere robots ... mechanical, unfeeling, uninspiring.

We are so driven by our own emotions, so captivated by our need to be right, that we fail to see the negative impact we create.

We think we're hiding our innermost fears from others. But the only thing we're successful at hiding is the truth from ourselves.

Unwittingly, we do and say things that push us even farther away from our dreams and goals. We act impulsively and narcissistically. We state our opinions forcefully. We become increasingly insensitive.

In this way, we *ourselves* make our goals increasingly unattainable. And so, we exacerbate our fears and anger and anxieties, like a spiral that keeps deepening.

A common malaise of the Information Age is burn-out.

That's because we are motivated to own as much as humanly possible.

Through your insight of Ecology, you already know that there is never an end in sight to such cravings. We can never own enough. And so, we find ourself on a constant roller coaster to achieve more and more and more. Inevitably, we burn out.

With the Wisdom of Magnanimity, you are motivated to see and understand the insecurities of the people around you.

Merely interjecting this perspective orchestrates you to look for ways to help them move beyond their insecurities.

The resulting decisions and actions end up making a difference in the lives of the people around you.

Your wisdom improves the quality of their lives.

For example, Walt Disney saw the insecurities in the people around him. This motivated him to create a fantasyland environment, like Disney Land and Disney World, where people could leave their worries behind, get refreshed and rejuvenated.

In the process, he built an empire and left behind a legacy.

L.L. Bean saw the insecurities in its customers. Customers, burned repeatedly by rip-off artists, were skeptical of buying through the mail. This motivated L.L. Bean to set up a now legendary money-back guarantee policy.

Making a difference in the lives of others is self-propelling.

When you work, you don't think of it as "work;" you think of it as fun, a hobby. It doesn't matter anymore how hard you work.

You are no longer driven *by* blind fear or blind ambition. You are driven *to* a loftier purpose.

You are no longer driven by how much money and power you can accumulate. You are driven by how much you can *contribute*.

This goal, this interest, this purpose, *overshadows* the inevitable tension and the worry and fear and burn-out that accompany it.

It unleashes the full force of your creativity and energy, thus propelling you to attain your exalted dreams.

Even though you don't directly pursue wealth accumulation, your wisdom creates it for you.

It's a Myth:

If it
feels good,
"just do it"

One of the results of the Information Age is the slogan, "If it feels good, do it!"

But this slogan is a bed of thorns.

Our feel-good times are always short-lived.

That's because, as we already know through the intelligence of Duality, good times and bad times come and go like waves in the ocean.

And any actions, words or thoughts based on in-the-moment feelings can't help but bring disappointment.

With the Wisdom of Magnanimity, you are so focused on the other person's insecurities that your ego vanishes.

Your need to be right evaporates.

You no longer have anything to prove.

You no longer have a need to display your talents or your competence.

And so, you approach the people around you with ordinariness and humility.

But you don't do it because you know that such behavior will ultimately bring you the rewards you desire.

You do it because it makes you feel *great*.

And that is the true essence of the Wisdom of Magnanimity.

You move from the feel-good mentality of the Information Age to the world of feeling great.

You see the world in a completely different way.

You realize that finding true love doesn't mean searching for the right partner. It means *becoming* a great partner.

Finding career success doesn't mean searching for the right employer. It means *becoming* a great employee.

Raising wonderful children doesn't mean bemoaning your fate with your "spoiled" children. It means *becoming* a great parent.

Leading a successful organization doesn't mean staffing with the best employees. It means *becoming* a great leader.

Changing the people around you doesn't mean lecturing and preaching to them. It means *becoming* a great person.

One of the myths perpetuated by the Information Age is that healthy relationships require a great deal of communication, listening, and negotiating.

Therapists insist that communication is vital to the success of our relationships and marriages.

Consultants train us that communication is essential to healthy team and boss-employee interactions.

This explains the flood of books, workshops and seminars that teach us communication techniques.

With the Wisdom of Magnanimity, you rise above mere techniques, tactics and ploys.

That's because Magnanimity introduces empathy and compassion into your interactions.

When compassion enters your vision, there isn't room left for ego or pettiness.

Your compassion crowds out any strong emotions you may otherwise experience, such as hurt or anger.

And this is the way it should be since most feelings of hurt and anger come from imagined differences rather than real differences.

The atmosphere between you gets charged with trust, love and implicit belief.

And with this rock-solid foundation, you partner together to communicate and resolve the few *real* disagreements — which are less than five percent of all disagreements.

Without Magnanimity, our life is immersed in petty irritations and disagreements. We are quick to harbor resentments.

When we communicate these irritations and resentments, the outcome is the *opposite* of what the therapists and consultants promise. That's because we only serve to alienate the other person and widen the chasm.

Each time we communicate *without* our wisdom, we undermine any remaining possibility of reconciliation.

We often end up losing everybody and everything we most value, including our self-esteem. While the authors, therapists, consultants — and often, attorneys — who sold us their advice end up collecting our money.

In the Information Age, we view the people in our life as though they were material possessions ... easily acquired and quickly disposed.

When a person behaves inappropriately, most of us are quick to judge, chastise, or even condemn that person.

Bosses are quick to fire employees. Lovers are quick to break up their relationships. Friends are quick to abandon their friends.

We never stop to consider the huge price we pay — in lost opportunities to learn and grow, in lost momentum, in lost investment — every time we recycle the people in our life.

With the spirit of Magnanimity, you almost immediately see that most inappropriate behavior stems from insecurity and so, it is usually a cry for attention.

Most parents look at a demanding child and attempt to suppress its inappropriate behavior.

With the Wisdom of Magnanimity, you see that the child is merely attempting to be seen and heard. So rather than chiding the child, you guide its search for independence within a framework of love, understanding and support.

Most people look at a feuding lover and see a person who is inconsiderate, selfish, perhaps even abusive and repulsive.

With the Wisdom of Magnanimity, you don't ignore any inappropriate behavior. But *first* you see straight through the noisy exterior to the inside. You see that your lover is afraid of not being loved enough, afraid of being abandoned, afraid of growing old alone.

Most bosses look at their uncooperative employees and complain about 'people problems.'

With the Wisdom of Magnanimity, you see that such employees are merely afraid of not being noticed, afraid of being passed over for a promotion, afraid that they'll be the target of the next lay-off.

Most salespeople get irritated when a potential customer asks too many questions before committing to buying a product.

With the Wisdom of Magnanimity, you see that your potential customer merely wants to feel secure that he won't get ripped off by you.

A wise gardener never gives up on a seedling just because it's struggling to gain a footing.

Instead, he looks for the one or two things that *he* can do — such as adding nutrients to the soil, changing the watering schedule, or perhaps re-sloping the land — to nurture the full-blown tree to emerge.

Similarly, with the acumen of Magnanimity, you look beyond the idiosyncrasies of the other person and you see his insecurities.

You see his enormous latent potential once he rises above his insecurities.

And you see what role *you* can play in helping him reach this unrealized potential.

In ninety percent of all cases, helping another individual bloom involves little more than a simple change in the situation and circumstance.

For example, with an uncooperative employee, it often means simply seeing the incompatibility between his capabilities and his job requirements ... and then, moving him to a function that takes advantage of his core competence.

With a skeptical customer, it often means simply recognizing his fear of being ripped-off ... and then, offering him an iron-clad, no-risk, money-back guarantee.

With a ranting boss, it often means simply allowing him the time to blow his steam.

With a disturbing lover, it often means simply providing a little bit of reassurance.

With an unsettled child, it often means simply showing him how much you believe in him.

All of these are small acts.

Even if they are not the "perfect" actions, your wisdom communicates that you *care*.

This builds the other person's sense of internal security. It also builds a sense of trust and confidence in you.

Which, in time, will engender substantial rewards for you.

Most people attempt to induce change by engaging the head.

They use logic and strategy.

But, with the Wisdom of Magnanimity, you see that change is not an intellectual exercise.

It is an emotional exercise.

Change intensifies the emotions of fear and insecurity.

So, you know that to induce change, you must engage the heart.

You must drive out the negative emotions of fear and insecurity and overpower them with the positive emotions of enthusiasm and wonder.

You use passion, purpose and dreams.

You show how, together, you can make a difference.

You become like a light that mesmerizes every moth in its vicinity.

You create a pathway for the others to follow.

And you light the pathway with your own personal passion, perseverance, courage, excitement and energy.

Instead of making it an obligation for others to follow you down the pathway, you create an *opportunity* for them to shine and glow ... just like you.

Instead of preaching the reasons why they should follow your lead, you *model* the way.

When Magnanimity engages your vision, it cements a bond between you and the people around you.

This applies equally to your relationships with friends, family, customers, employees, shareholders.

In the world of business, this bond pays off big, long-term dividends, whether your business is small or large, private or public.

For example, Sam Walton could see the insecurities of customers. So, he positioned greeters at the doors of his Wal-Mart stores to make the customers feel warm and welcome, and also to point out specific departments to customers who may be afraid of getting lost in the massive maze of his stores.

Walton could see the insecurities of customers afraid of approaching a salesperson or being "sold" by a salesperson. So, he implemented the "Ten-foot rule." This rule requires every sales person to greet any customer who gets within ten feet of him and help the customer feel warm and secure.

It is this vision of enhancing the customer's experience that has made the strongest contribution to Wal-Mart's meteoric rise — not, as is commonly believed, the large variety and the discount prices.

When we view customers *without* our wisdom engaged, we make foolish choices that erode our customer base.

For example, AT&T is quick to offer deals to customers of other long distance carriers to entice them into switching. They heavily promote their best deals to new prospects. Yet, existing customers have to *know* to ask for the best deal; otherwise they keep paying the older, higher prices, month after month.

With this practice, AT&T is actually intensifying the fears and anxieties of its existing customer base who wonder whether they're being taken for a ride. The long-term effect of this loss of wisdom is proving disastrous to the company's profitability.

When Magnanimity is combined with Aggregation, it leads to a deep understanding of your customer's needs.

And when your actions are based on your customer's needs, it triggers a chain reaction of higher sales.

This is how the potent combination of Magnanimity and Aggregation works:

As you see your customer's fears and anxieties and needs, you clearly understand what problem he's trying to solve.

Then, with your Wisdom of Aggregation, you design precise solutions that fit your customer's individual problem like a glove.

For example, a customer comes to your store to buy a hand wrench.

Most of us have blinders on and so, we focus on that one single transaction.

But with your combined wisdom, you look at the broader picture and realize that your customer is really working on a progressive project to remodel his kitchen. As a result, you see an opportunity most others wouldn't see.

Once you see this opportunity, you don't get dollar signs in your eyes and move in for the kill.

You maintain a broader, more empathetic perspective. You take the time to see exactly what your customer has in mind for his project and you partner with him, seeing more and more of his *individual* needs.

As you bring in your expertise to help him fulfill these specific needs and allay his fears of completing his task on time and on budget, you effectively shut off your competitors ... for life.

As you can see, your combined wisdom creates your wealth ... for life.

The Information Age distorts our perspective about what it takes to forge ahead in the real world.

It leads us to believe that the fastest way to move forward is to introduce new products and new technologies.

The Wisdom of Magnanimity alters your perspective.

It helps you see that the most effective way for forging ahead comes, not from new products or new technologies, but from new ways of interacting with people.

And all these new ways of interacting with people are invariably centered around allaying people's fears and anxieties.

For example, most companies are in a mad rush to install the latest computers, the breakthrough technologies, the fastest gadgets.

But the companies that get these new gizmos to *produce results* are the ones that take the time to allay the fears of the employees — who are naturally concerned about their future.

The specific *way* in which these companies address these fears is not important. There are as many different ways as there are consultants.

But the fact that the company has the wisdom to *take the time* tells the employees that the company *cares*. And so, such companies, even with not-so-new technologies, are able to outstrip their competition.

Microsoft has rarely been first on the market with anything. Its Windows operating system is based on the Macintosh operating system. Its Excel spreadsheet followed Lotus. For office networks of computers, it followed Novell's lead.

Yet, Microsoft is able to snatch the lead position away from everyone it follows simply because it ably addresses customers' most nagging questions, "Will my new software be compatible with what I already own? If I upgrade my software, will everything still work together?"

As you can see, how you see the world changes how the world sees you.

123

Accessing
THE WISDOM OF MAGNANIMITY

(1)   Today, I will reflect on how I look at all the people I encounter every day. Do I really *see* their insecurities, their fears, their needs? Do I act in a way that acknowledges their insecurities? Do I feel love and compassion for the suffering I know they're experiencing?

(2)   Today, I will also reflect on my own goals, fears and obstacles. Do I allow these feelings to take center stage so that they reduce my ability to connect with reality and with the fears of the people around me?

(3)   Today, I will also reflect on what really drives me. Am I on a mission to accumulate more things, more possessions? Or, am I moving forward towards partnering with others to help them move beyond their insecurities?

The Wisdom

of

Stratification

Nature showers you with an overabundance
of information and tasks.

Yet when you see through this clutter
with one-pointed attention,
each moment becomes
abundantly fruitful
and completely worthwhile.

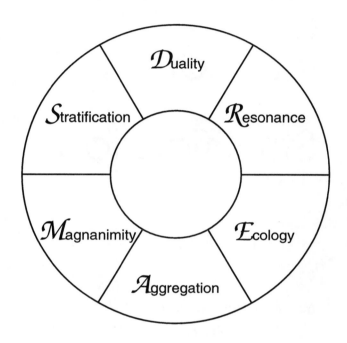

*The butterfly
counts not months
but moments,*

and has time enough

Rabindranath Tagore

The Wisdom of Stratification is the sixth wisdom to awaken inside you.

Stratification comes from the word *Stratify,* which means "to separate into layers."

And with the Wisdom of Stratification, you stratify the clutter of tasks and information in front of you. To do this, simply look at your tasks in aggregate. And your wisdom will pinpoint your most effective task.

Then, *give this task your unwavering attention.*

With the five prior wisdoms, you gained perspective and learned to see the world around you in a new light.

This sixth wisdom is your springboard for *action.*

Nothing happens without action.

But it is important to remember that the quality of your actions governs the quality of your results.

Stratification focuses your attention on the actions that bring you the results you desire in the most effective way possible.

In the Information Age, we suffer from Hummingbird Syndrome. Like a hummingbird, we constantly flit from one flower to the next, trying to visit the maximum number of flowers. We mistake activity for productivity. We never stop long enough at any one flower to make a difference.

With the Wisdom of Stratification, you see things differently.

Like an eagle hunting for prey, you survey your landscape in aggregate. Then, once you identify the specific location of your prey, you swoop down, your focus unwaveringly on the task in front of you.

At the bottom line, *how you see* what you're doing is what really matters.

Stratification doesn't mean you shut off your Wisdom of Aggregation. Once you turn on the light to see things in aggregate, *that light stays on.*

Even as the eagle swoops down, it remains aware of the landscape in aggregate ... just in case the target moves.

The symbol of the Wisdom of Stratification is the magnifying glass.

A magnifying glass has the incredible power to capture the otherwise harmless rays of the sun and focus its light energy with such intensity that it burns a hole through a piece of paper.

Similarly, your metaphorical magnifying glass accumulates your otherwise disbursed energy and focuses it with such extraordinary energy that you collect extraordinary payback.

When your energy is scattered, everything around you whithers, weakens and ultimately vanishes.

But once your wisdom focuses your energy, both your results and your relationships become as solid as a rock.

The Wisdom of Stratification has two components.

The first component builds upon your Wisdom of Magnanimity. The second component builds upon your Wisdom of Aggregation.

The first component solidifies your relationships. The second component guarantees your results.

With the Wisdom of Magnanimity, you learned to see the insecurities and the sufferings of the people who dot your landscape.

Now with Stratification, you narrow your focus to the specific individual in front of you ... and look at it him as though he were the most important person you'll encounter during the day.

With the Wisdom of Aggregation, you learned to see the patterns that interconnect the information and events around you.

Now with Stratification, you narrow your focus to a specific *optimum* piece of the pattern ... and look at it as though it were the most important task you'll encounter during the day.

During any particular day or period of time, you may have many balls in the air. You may have many tasks to complete. You may have many people to interact with.

And you may actually devote barely a few minutes to each task or to each individual.

But with the Wisdom of Stratification, you see each moment with undivided attention.

And this focus, this cognizance, this one-pointed attention makes each moment — and all the moments that follow it — completely worthwhile.

YOUR MOST
IMPORTANT TASK

The Information Age makes it possible for us to do more than one thing at the same time.

And so, we listen to the radio *and* drive at the same time. We talk on the telephone *and* drive. We shave *and* drive. We nurture our kids *and* drive them to school.

Technology was intended to make us more effective.

But, by making it possible for us to dilute and split our attention in this way, technology has inadvertently made us _in_effective.

For example, many time-pressed, career parents think of the time they drive their kids to school as a good substitute for the "quality time" they should spend with their child.

Such parents feel a sense of efficiency and accomplishment, because they think they've killed two birds with one stone.

But Stratification reveals that such feelings are doomed to be short-lived. That's because the child is deprived of true, meaningful, intimate quality time. So, it starts acting up, by misbehaving, missing school, or even taking up drugs. This demands an inordinate amount of time from the parent, and ultimately overshadows the time the parent saved up front.

When an employee knocks on the door, many managers invite the employee in to talk. But *they continue to work.*

Stratification reveals that such inattention will send the employee the impression that whatever grieves him is not important enough.

So, the employee will hesitate to return the next time he has a grievance. So will other employees who hear of the first employee's experience. In this way, a simple lack of attention can eat through the company like a cancer, triggering low morale and low productivity, ultimately debilitating the company.

Through the technological wonder of call-waiting, it is now possible for us to answer a call in the midst of a conversation with another person.

But Stratification reveals that when we divide our attention in this way, we don't do justice to either person … or to ourselves.

When we interrupt a conversation, we send a strong signal to the person we interrupted that we don't consider him important enough.

We also send a strong signal to the person whose call we answered that we won't stop in the future to cut *him* off in the same way.

It's a Myth:

You can
walk
and
chew gum
at
the same time

When we operate without the Wisdom of Stratification, we live in delusion.

We believe we're becoming efficient. But in reality, we become increasingly ineffective.

In our struggle to get more done in less time and clean our plate, we inadvertently cause our plate to get piled even higher.

What starts out as a little bit of inattention mushrooms into a cloud of chaos and grief.

Ultimately, we lose sight of what caused our grief in the first place and blame our misery on our environment and other people.

On the other hand, as you embody your vision with the Wisdom of Stratification, you find yourself accomplishing everything your heart desires, without friction and without significant effort.

That's because your accumulated wisdom infuses you with a glow that mesmerizes everyone around you.

Through the exquisite combination of Duality, Magnanimity and Stratification, you get bestowed with a powerful charisma.

Duality provides the foundation for this magnetism. Because with it, you see the people around you as equal to yourself. You view yourself with self-assurance and you view others with belief and confidence.

Magnanimity provides the structure for this sparkle. Because with it, you view the people around you with the deepest respect, empathy and understanding.

And Stratification fortifies your power. Because with it, you view each person in front of you as the most important person of the moment.

These three wisdoms don't involve much doing or saying. What you do or say comes as a direct result of how you see.

So, once these three wisdoms are merged together in how you see others, there isn't much need to do or say anything. Your charisma becomes effortless and the attainment of your goals becomes spontaneous.

It's important to keep in mind that you can't *work* at becoming charismatic. Your goal can't be to patronize others or manipulate them. And you can't assume a sense of false humility. Your charisma is merely a joyous side-benefit of awakening your wisdom.

Scientists have proven that over 90% of all communication is nonverbal.

And through the Wisdoms of Magnanimity and Stratification, you know that all nonverbal communications stem specifically from how you *see* the other person.

Ultimately, how you see the other person determines your posture, your inflection, your tone.

Despite this fundamental reality, the Information Age is sweeping us rapidly towards a world where the emphasis of communications is words … rather than sight, vision, or perception.

Computers and telecommunications are making it possible for us to transmit large quantities of *words* at ever-faster speeds.

Technology is seducing us into believing that we can dispense with the essential nonverbal part of our communications.

Unfortunately, when we forego the nonverbal part of our communications, we also sacrifice our relationships.

With Stratification, you place a heavy emphasis on communicating to the other person how important he/she is to you.

So, you place a heavy emphasis on face-to-face communications. You delegate only routine, *non-interactive* communications to e-mail or voice mail.

Most people would complain that reducing your reliance on e-mail and voice mail would drastically reduce the efficiency of your communications.

But with Stratification, your goal is not to increase the *efficiency* of your communications.

It is to increase the *effectiveness* of your relationships.

Your goal is not to get connected to a lot of people.

It is to *connect with* the people in your life.

At its heart, Stratification is about relationships and results ... about connecting and creating.

In the Information Age, we try to create results by identifying tasks and then, scheduling them in our planners or to-do lists.

But we typically fail to complete most of these tasks. Because it is nature's way to always give us more tasks than it's possible to complete.

And so, we get enveloped in gnawing guilt.

With Stratification, your focus is on making each moment worthwhile.

So, you tap your Wisdom of Aggregation to identify the few tasks that are most critical to fulfilling your goals and ideologies.

Then, you focus unwaveringly on each of these tasks.

As a result, you make substantial progress, while others are still drowning under their mountain of tasks.

For example, when scheduling a manufacturing company, most people get inundated with tasks such as perfecting the paperwork, scheduling the step-by-step operations, getting accurate inventory status, collecting accurate labor costs.

With Aggregation and Stratification, you see that, although all these tasks are important, they pale in comparison to the task of making sure you have adequate capacity to accomplish your overall schedules. Without adequate capacity, none of the details are significant. While with adequate capacity, many of the details take care of themselves.

Similarly, many companies spend an inordinate amount of time examining the flow of parts and paperwork with a view to cut costs and cycle time.

With Aggregation and Stratification, you recognize that the bulk of your time and costs are tied in the variety and complexity of your product design.

So, if your goal is to slash costs, you attack product design before you tackle process flow. You see that removing the complexity and variety from your product design will, in itself, improve process flow.

Stratification goes beyond focusing on the layers that are most productive at creating results.

It also requires *de*-focusing on the layers that are unproductive.

So, you don't just look for the key tasks to do. You look with equal vigor for the tasks and initiatives to *not* do.

For example, on a personal level, when most people have a grievance about something, they spend a lot of time fuming, feeling depressed, and awfulizing to their family and co-workers.

Some people even go to their therapists to complain about the injustice they're suffering.

With Stratification, you see at once that none of these conversations — with yourself, your friends, or your therapist — are worthwhile. The only worthwhile conversation is the one with the person who can *do something* about what bothers you. So, you stop wasting your time and breath ... and talk it over with the person who can make a difference.

Most companies set up elaborate systems to track and count inventory. But having such a system actually *encourages* building inventory. And, inventory in excess of what you need, increases both costs and lead time.

With Stratification, you see that by simply eliminating the system and facility for storing inventory, you disallow the building of inventory. Thus, you dramatically cut costs and cycle times. You can also completely eliminate the entire support crew required to maintain the elaborate systems.

Very often, when you decide to *stop* doing something, you create a far more powerful impact than anything new you *start* doing.

Many companies continue doing a task, or following a procedure, or selling a product long after its original need has expired and been forgotten. They fail to see that *stopping* such tasks, procedures or products can free up much-needed resources and thus, make it *easier* to accomplish their current goals.

In the Information Age, tasks and effort and information command so much of our time that we've come to believe that the moments that are *void* of tasks and information are the most fulfilling.

So, we crave leisure time. We actively cut corners to get to our goals faster so that we may enjoy our "free time."

Our entire attention is focused on getting to that elusive stage of nothingness as quickly as possible.

But we seek happiness where happiness can't be found.

When we finally reach that stage where we are work-free and worry-free, we realize with a flash that this stage is only temporary. We wonder, "Is that all?" We crave, "I want more." Eventually, we sink into a deep feeling of emptiness.

With the Wisdom of Stratification, you focus on making each moment worthwhile.

You look for ways to make the moment more effective, more productive. You look for ways to harness your best resources.

You get so immersed in the moment that there's no room in your vision for distractions or emotions.

In a sense, you *create* each moment.

And, in the process, you create your own joy, ecstacy and fulfillment.

With Stratification, you start out by looking with an intense passion at the task in front of you.

But once you start your task, you also become able to see *what to do next*.

Conventional wisdom has taught us to think before we act.

YOUR NEXT STEP

But, in the Age of Wisdom, when you act — and pay attention to your action — you boost your ability to think.

In other words, your Wisdom of Stratification boosts your ability to see things in aggregate.

This is especially critical in today's world where so much is changing so fast that sometimes it's difficult to clearly see things in aggregate.

New solutions and new technologies emerge every day. Consumer tastes and savvy get constantly redefined.

Sometimes, it's difficult to see what will stick, what will hold, what will fall off today, what will fall off tomorrow.

Sometimes, it's difficult to see whether what worked yesterday will work tomorrow.

With Stratification, the huge, unknown void in front of you doesn't faze you.

Because you recognize that once you start moving forward, the rest of the path will become readily visible to you, just as reflective road markers become progressively visible on a fogged-in highway.

All you have to do is keep your eyes open and allow your collective wisdom to shine the light for you.

Most people are not in touch with their own wisdom. So, they don't trust their wisdom to guide them. They seek out perfectly visible pathways. They're afraid to experiment.

So, they get left behind, even as you make major inroads towards your goals.

Accessing
THE WISDOM OF STRATIFICATION

(1)   Today, I will reflect on the following issues ... when I interact with another person, do I treat him or her as the most important person I'll meet that day?

(2)   When I work on a task, do I do it with one-pointed attention?

(3)   If I'm not sure of what to do next, do I move forward anyway, relying on my collective wisdom to make the subsequent step obvious to me?

The Wisdom

of

Enlightenment

Every individual and every event
that enters your life
contains the seeds of a vital life lesson.

And when you see this lesson
and allow its wisdom to sprout freely,
you experience
the ultimate and inevitable
attainment of your goals.

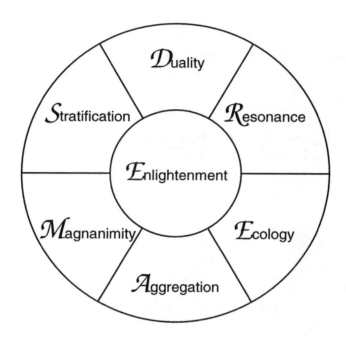

Education gives you

neither experience

nor wisdom.

Peter Drucker

The Wisdom of Enlightenment switches on the seventh light in the room of your mind.

It is the seventh and final nudge to wake up your wisdom so that you can see the world in a new way.

Think of the seven wisdoms as the seven colors of the rainbow spectrum. At the end of this seventh step, when all seven colors are lit, lies the combined effect of all seven colors ... *enlightenment*.

The seven colors of the rainbow interact dynamically to help you see things the way they really are.

In the same way, the Wisdom of Enlightenment invigorates the other wisdoms so that you can see your world as it really is.

The symbol of the Wisdom of Enlightenment is the rainbow. The symbol represents seeing all the seven colors distinctly. It also represents seeing the magic that gets created when you see the seven colors integrated.

The word *Enlightened* means to be informed, to be illuminated, to be freed from ignorance, to engage in *learning*.

And the Wisdom of Enlightenment is about seeing what you can learn ... and learning from what you see.

In the Information Age, we have a flawed view of learning.

We mistake education and experience and knowledge for learning.

So, we accumulate a lot of education and a lot of experience. We stack our resumes with degrees and titles and association and club memberships.

We also accumulate a lot of information. We read books, attend seminars, browse the internet.

With the Wisdom of Enlightenment, you know that, in order to learn, you must *process* your education, your experience, your knowledge.

Data is useless until it is processed and transformed into information. In the same way, education, experience, knowledge and information are useless until they are processed and transformed into learning.

Learning is not about techniques or how-to-do-it formulas; it's about thinking, reflecting, musing, considering, exploring — even imagining — with a view to enhancing your wisdom.

For example, many people go to seminars and workshops to learn "better listening" techniques.

But listening is much more than patiently hearing what the other person has to say. It is much more than cueing the other person to speak up.

Listening is about sincerely *caring* about what's *happening* to the other person.

It's about *seeing* the other person through your Wisdoms of Magnanimity and Stratification.

At the bottom line, listening is not about technique. It's about changing the way you see.

Learning about listening is not about adding a new skill to your bag of skills. It's about examining and re-orienting the way you see the people in your life.

In a similar vein, many of us take pride in our years of experience in a particular job or profession.

But learning is much more than accumulating time on the job. It is about seeing the patterns that interconnect all the people, information and events. It is, once again, about changing the way you see.

With the Wisdom of Enlightenment, you look for a learning opportunity in everything that you do and in everything that happens around you.

It's a Myth:

Experience
is
the best teacher

Knowledge, education and experience have a habit of making people who acquire them arrogant.

But true wisdom leads to humility and respect, not arrogance.

That's because each time you learn, you learn how much more there is yet to learn.

Yet, unlike most people, you don't get overwhelmed by how much there is to learn.

Because you focus your learning, not on techniques or programs or formulas, but on enhancing your ability to see, to be resourceful and to access your wisdom.

You focus your learning on improving your ability to see things *as they really are.*

With your Wisdom of Enlightenment, each time you learn, you also learn how much you have to <u>un</u>learn.

That's because of the should's and shouldn'ts and the do's and don'ts that have been passed down over the years by your parents, gurus, teachers and experts.

These "rules" and "answers" form opaque barriers between you and the true reality. They prevent you from truly *seeing.*

Now with your Wisdom of Enlightenment, you see that they also prevent you from truly learning.

For example, if John Peterman had not *un*learned everything the experts told him was vital for a successful clothing catalog, he would have never seen the way to create a revolutionary, new catalog design.

But Peterman was willing to look past the artificial barriers of the do's and don'ts from the experts (Duality).

He looked for the true key to success for *his* catalog company, and discovered that even though he couldn't afford a full-size catalog, even though he couldn't afford photographs, he could compensate by romancing his customers with artistic sketches and poetic musings (Aggregation).

He took the first small, but important, step. And he bestowed undistracted attention on this step to see what more he could learn (Stratification and Enlightenment).

As a result, he gathered accolades for his company and huge rewards for himself personally.

When we fail to process our knowledge and experience, we become our own worst enemy.

We look for answers where answers cannot be found.

We drown in a sea of babble from self-proclaimed experts.

We get tossed around as fads come and go.

Ultimately, we lose faith in our own abilities and even in our innate wisdom.

What we forget is that nature has bestowed each of us with infinite wisdom. And our wisdom is incapable of failing us. But we do have to wake up and tap our wisdom.

Consider an individual eager to start a successful business. He wades through a sea of books and information and determines that authors and experts alike preach that having a well-thought-out business plan is the key to a successful business.

So, he "learns" as much about planning as he possibly can. Then, he confidently applies his newly-acquired "skills" to his start-up.

But his business fails nevertheless.

And that's because he failed to process his knowledge through his internal Wisdom.

Had he seen business planning through his Wisdom of Duality, he would have seen immediately that there are times when business planning is good, and there are times when business planning actually *makes things worse!*

Had he seen planning through his Wisdom of Stratification, he would have seen that, when you're unclear about exactly how to proceed, the most important thing to do is to take the next step … and then, learn from that step.

Had he seen planning through his Wisdom of Aggregation, he would have seen that, even if he put together a business plan, he'd have to be willing to give up this initial strategy entirely if the circumstances changed.

In the Information Age, we wish everything in the world obeys the laws of Physics.

In Physics, the laws are straightforward and logical. Drop an apple and it falls due to the force of gravity. Apply pressure to something and it will exert an equal and opposite pressure back. You can explain everything with formulas and equations.

In the Age of Wisdom, you see the world through the eyes of a Biologist or an Astronomer.

You know that the world is so complex, so infinite that you can never map it completely. The best you can do is ascertain the patterns, interpret them and extrapolate from them (Aggregation).

Astronomers locate distant stars not by actually seeing them. But by seeing the distortions in light and energy around the location and extrapolating from this information.

Doctors diagnose patients not by actually seeing the ailment. But by discerning the symptoms and extrapolating from this information.

Because of the complexity of the system they're dealing with, doctors and astronomers know to continuously and simultaneously access their Wisdoms of Aggregation, Stratification and Enlightenment.

With Aggregation, they make an initial diagnosis, based on the patterns they're first able to see.

With Stratification, they move one step forward and pay religious attention to that step. Doctors prescribe a treatment. Astronomers assign an initial location.

Then with Enlightenment, they see what they can learn from this step to fine-tune their initial interpretation. They also see how they can learn to make better interpretations with all future endeavors.

At its heart, the Wisdom of Enlightenment is about constantly sharpening your ability to see and interpret reality.

You start by seeing what you can learn.

You end up learning simply because you're willing to see.

In the Information Age, appearances are so important that we are programmed from a very early age to hide our mistakes.

As children, we learn to hide our mistakes from our class mates, parents and teachers.

As employees, we learn to hide our mistakes from our boss and co-workers.

As leaders and executives, we learn to hide our mistakes from our employees, stockholders, customers, competitors.

Unfortunately, as we scurry to hide these mistakes from others, we end up also hiding these mistakes from ourselves.

And so, we miss out on the biggest learning opportunity.

With the Wisdom of Enlightenment, you look at mistakes as your opportunity to learn and grow. Rather than hiding them from yourself, you look at them, inspect them, review them ... and use the learning to wake up your wisdom.

Sooner or later, everyone gets fired from a job, or gets dumped by a lover, or loses a major contract from a customer.

But when most people face such an experience, they tend to flee. Or, they look for someone to blame.

With the Wisdom of Enlightenment, you see what you can learn from every experience.

So, in honor of your own learning, you swallow your pride, and patiently learn from your firing employer, or your dumping lover, or your cutting-off customer.

You learn about yourself, your learn which wisdom within you still needs a nudge, and then you go about patiently rethinking the way you see and the way you think.

In the Information Age, it is fashionable to study the past. Some of us do it because we are nostalgic. Others do it because we're curious. Still others do it because we're interested in history.

With the Wisdom of Enlightenment, you pay attention to the past to understand, reflect on, and marvel at the timelessness of wisdom.

You see the lives of legends such as Mahatma Gandhi, Martin Luther King, Confucius, Mozart, Galileo, Socrates, Gautama Buddha to understand the impact they made in the past and the impact they continue to make today.

You also reflect on how you can make a similar impact on your world yourself.

It is the way of human nature to interpret the world around us as we'd like it to be, rather than the way it really is.

It is also the way of human nature to attempt to change the world around us to *become* the way we'd like it to be.

This is why, in the Information Age, most people can't resist the temptation to change the people around them.

For example, parents try to coax their children into becoming more outgoing.

Partners try to to change their lovers into becoming more communicative.

Bosses try to change their employees into being more organized.

With the Wisdom of Duality, you already know to accept and acknowledge and appreciate the people around you *just the way they are.*

You know to cherish them for who they are, rather than for who you'd like them to be.

And the kindest, most benevolent gift you can give to another person is to help him preserve his uniqueness while, at the same time, helping him see the world as it really is.

In other words, to help him enlighten himself, help him wake up his own wisdom, and thus, allow the best from within him to emerge.

And to do all of this without allowing your own biases, judgements or interpretations to interfere.

Helping another person wake up and truly see is a magical, indescribable experience.

And it's magical not just because of the effect it has on the other person.

It's magical because of the effect it has on you.

The process of enlightening another person ends up enlightening you as well.

You end up see the Duality more vividly, the Resonance more certainly, the Ecology more perceptibly, the Aggregation more distinctly, the Magnanimity more empathetically, the Stratification more pronouncedly.

In the end, the teacher becomes the student. And the student becomes the teacher.

Accessing
THE WISDOM OF ENLIGHTENMENT

(1)   Today, I will reflect on how I process all my knowledge and education and experience. In everything that happens around me, do I see what I can learn? Do I learn from what I see? Do I reflect, think, understand, imagine, with a view to waking up my wisdom?

(2)   Is my newfound wisdom making me more humble and more compassionate? If not, why not?

(3)   Do I look for ways to enlighten people around me in a way that allows the best from within them to emerge?

Conclusion

No one can give you wisdom.

Your wisdom is uniquely your own.

You were born with it.

But, until you read this book, you were perhaps not aware of its infinite power.

My goal with this book has been to make you aware of your in-born wisdom, help you nudge it awake, and then, use it as the cornerstone of everything you do, everything you say, to everyone in your life.

With each wisdom, I've attempted to shed the light on different aspects of life so that you can see how to use your own wisdom to pilot your life.

As you have seen, wisdom is not about doing things differently. It is about seeing things differently. And by seeing things differently, you end up doing things differently ... which ultimately leads to a sense of abiding joy in your life.

The most important aspect of waking up your wisdom is that you rise above the emotions of fear, insecurity, and anxiety.

Yet paradoxically, you also become a more emotional person, because you connect with others emotionally.

You also find yourself speaking less as you learn to observe more.

Yet once again paradoxically, because of your deep wisdom, you find people seeking you to hear your thoughts.

There are very few people who see and think clearly.

There are even fewer people who see and think clearly all the time.

This is not because they're not able to do so. But because they are not aware that they *can* do so. My hope, with this book is that you see that *you* can do so.

Once you get started on the journey of seeing things as they really are, you'll find that it becomes more and more effortless.

Because, ultimately, wisdom is effortless.

People with a fully awakened wisdom have a unique perspective of the world.

They look at everything that comes into their life — including talent, money and people — with a sense of gratitude and responsibility.

They look at themselves, not as owners, but as guardians of the people, possessions that come into their lives.

They look for ways to make a difference, to leave everything they encounter better than how they found it.

With people, they look for ways to make them feel accepted (Duality) and secure (Magnanimity).

With time, they look for ways to make the most of it (Stratification).

With talent, they look for ways to make it flower (Enlightenment).

With money, they look for ways to multiply it (Aggregation).

Now go, make a difference — in your life and in the world.